T0258330

The Hypochondriac

adapted by Roger McGough

Methuen Drama

Published by Methuen Drama 2009

1 3 5 7 9 10 8 6 4 2

Methuen Drama
A & C Black Publishers Limited
36 Soho Square
London W1D 3QY
www.acblack.com

A CIP catalogue record for this book is available
from the British Library

ISBN: 978 1 408 12385 0

Typeset by Country Setting, Kingsdown, Kent
Printed and bound in Great Britain by
CPI Cox & Wyman, Reading, Berkshire

Liverpool Everyman and Playhouse and English Touring
Theatre present Roger McGough's new adaptation of
Molière's The Hypochondriac

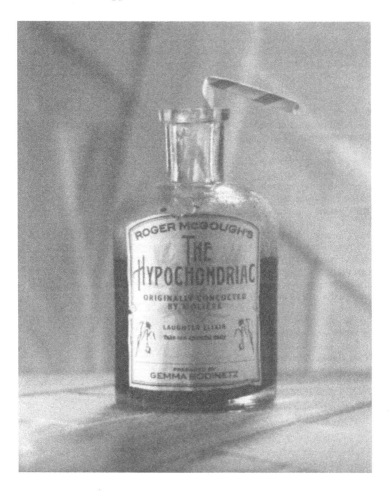

First performed on 19 June 2009
at the Liverpool Playhouse Theatre

Production
sponsored by

About the Everyman and Playhouse

Liverpool Everyman and Playhouse together make up a single engine for creative excellence, artistic adventure and audience involvement. Since 1999 the theatres have been on a remarkable journey, described as "a theatrical renaissance on Merseyside" (Observer). An integrated programme across the two buildings has generated critical acclaim and audience growth, and has been the springboard for forward-looking programmes of artist development and youth and community engagement.

In recent years our work has been enjoyed beyond the city, with transfers to London and Edinburgh, as well as tours around the country. These have included productions of *Yellowman*, *The Anniversary*, the award-winning *Unprotected* and *The Snow Queen* (with Teatro Kismet). In 2008, as part of our celebrations as European Capital of Culture, we co produced *3 Sisters* on *Hope Street* with Hampstead Theatre, transferred a new version of *Tartuffe* by Roger McGough to Kingston's Rose Theatre, co-produced *Boeing-Boeing* for a national tour and welcomed Pete Postlethwaite back to the Everyman with *King Lear*, a co production with Headlong and the Young Vic.

But there is more to these theatres than simply the work on our stages. We have a busy Literary Department, working to nurture the next generation of Liverpool Playwrights. A wide-ranging Community Department takes our work to all corners of the city and surrounding areas, and works in partnership with schools, colleges, youth and community groups to open up the theatre to all.

To find out more about our work, both on and off stage, call 0151 709 4776 or visit www.everymanplayhouse.com

Two Great Theatres. One Creative Heart.

Liverpool Everyman and Playhouse is a registered charity No.1081229

Our Funders

Production sponsored by
Liverpool John Moores University

The ethos of Liverpool John Moores University is summed up in three simple words – Dream Plan Achieve – reflecting our commitment to eradicating the poverty of aspiration that stops many people from achieving their full potential. Following our sponsorship of *Tartuffe* last year, we are delighted to sponsor this new adaptation by LJMU Fellow, Roger McGough. At LJMU we are committed, through partnership and enterprise, to positively impacting on social and cultural advancement at local, national and international levels. Our support and relationship with the Everyman and Playhouse is a perfect reflection of this commitment.

ETT

ENGLISH TOURING THEATRE

Surprise • Delight • Enrich • Engage

Under the direction of Rachel Tackley, ETT presents potent, vivid and
vital productions of new and classic plays to audiences far and wide.
A powerhouse of touring theatre, ETT works with a rich and varied mix
of the country's leading directors, actors and artists to stage thrilling and
ambitious theatre that is vigorous, popular and, above all, entertaining.

Visit us at www.ett.org.uk or e-mail us at admin@ett.org.uk

ETT in 2009:

Been So Long

A new musical by Che Walker, music by Arthur
Darvill; produced with the Young Vic

Young Vic 11th June – 15th July
Latitude Festival 17th/18th July
Traverse Theatre, Edinburgh 7th – 30th August

The Hypochondriac

By Molière in a new translation by Roger McGough;
produced with Liverpool Everyman Playhouse

UK Tour 15th September – 14th November

The Grapes of Wrath

Adapted from John Steinbeck's novel by Frank Galati;
produced with Chichester Festival Theatre

Chichester Festival Theatre 10th July – 28th August
UK Tour 1st October – 21st November

Credits

Cast (in alphabetical order)

Leanne Best	Toinette
Neil Caple	Diaforius
Simon Coates	Beralde
Toby Dantzic	Thomas
Clive Francis	Argan
Jake Harders	Cleante
Chris Porter	Bonnefoi, Monsieur Fleurant, Doctor Purgeon
Lucinda Raikes	Angelique
Brigid Zengeni	Beline

Other parts played by members of the company

Writer	Molière
Adaptor	Roger McGough
Director	Gemma Bodinetz
Designer	Mike Britton
Composer	Conor Linehan
Lighting Designer	Charles Balfour
Sound Designer	Jason Barnes
Movement Director	Bernadette Iglich
Costume Supervisor	Jacquie Davies
Casting Director	Ginny Schiller
Associate Director	Lisa Spirling
Production Manager (Liverpool)	Sean Pritchard
Production Manager (Tour)	Felix Davies
Company Manager	Paul Sawtell
Stage Manager	Natalia Cortes
Deputy Stage Manager	Roxanne Vella
Assistant Stage Manager	Helen Wilson
Lighting and Sound operators	Jennifer Tallon Cahill Lizzie Moran
Stage Crew	Jason McQuaide Mike Grey
Dresser	Kate Foster
Cover Image	Uniform

The company wishes to thank:

Ludlow Book Binders

Cast

Leanne Best
Toinette

Neil Caple
Diaforius

Leanne's theatre credits include:
Horse Marines (Plymouth Theatre
Royal's Drum); *Drowning On Dry
Land* (Salisbury Playhouse);
Desperately Seeking Susan (Novello
Theatre); *Unprotected* (Traverse
Theatre); *34* (Fecund Theatre Company);
The Way Home, The Morris and
Unprotected (Liverpool Everyman);
Solitary Confinement (King's Head
Theatre); *Our Country's Good, The Flint
Street Nativity* and *Popcorn* (Liverpool
Playhouse).

Television credits include:
*Casualty, Heatwave, Wire in the
Blood, Memory of Water, Casbah
– A Documentary, New Street Law,
Mobile* and *Moving On.*

Radio credits include:
*The Importance of Being Earnest,
Hen Night, Brief Lives* and *Writing
The Century.*

Film credits include:
Choices and *The Be All And
The End All.*

Neil's theatre credits include:
Billy Wonderful (Liverpool Everyman);
Unprotected (Liverpool Everyman and
Traverse, Edinburgh); *The Servant of
Two Masters, The Warehouse, The Flint
Street Nativity, Breezeblock Park* and *The
Odd Couple* (Liverpool Playhouse); *Lost
Soul, On the Ledge* and *Two* (Royal Court,
Liverpool); *Othello* (Watermill Theatre
Company and Tokyo); *The Merry Wives
of Windsor, The Wind In The Willows, The
Trackers of Oxyrynchus and Strangeways*
(Royal National Theatre); *A Comedy of
Errors* and *Macbeth* (Royal Shakespeare
Company); *The Front Page* (Donmar
Warehouse); *Much Ado About Nothing*
and *Julius Caesar* (Regents Park) and
Waterland (Shaw).

Television credits include:
*Far from the Madding Crowd, Cadfael, The
Bullion Boys, Civvies, Casualty, Holby City,
The Bill, Coronation St, Brookside, Doctors,
Pygmalion, Lee & Herring's Fist of Fun.*

Radio credits include:
Neil has appeared in over 20 plays for
Radio 4, read the *Morning Story* and
been a regular on *Weekending.*

Film credits include:
Rebecca's Daughters and *No Way Out!*

Cast

Simon Coates
Beralde

Toby Dantzic
Thomas

Simon's theatre credits include:
The Real Thing (The Gate Theatre,
Dublin); *Wuthering Heights*
(Birmingham Rep); *Tartuffe* (Liverpool
Playhouse and The Rose Theatre,
Kingston); *Black Snow, Arturo Ui,
Pygmalion, Murmuring Judges, Macbeth,
Arcadia, A Midsummer Night's Dream*
and *Translations* (National Theatre);
As You Like It (Cheek By Jowl – Olivier
Award nomination for Best Supporting
Actor, New York Drama Desk Award
nomination for Outstanding Featured
Actor); *The Comedy of Errors, The
Taming of the Shrew, Luminosity,
Loveplay, The Merry Wives of Windsor*
and *Coriolanus* (Royal Shakespeare
Company); *Hand in Hand* and *Life
After Scandal* (Hampstead Theatre)
and *The Constant Wife* (The Gate
Theatre, Dublin).

Television credits include:
*Eastenders, A Touch of Frost, The Bill,
The Amazing Mrs Pritchard* and
Dream Team.

Toby's theatre credits include:
Wuthering Heights (Birmingham Rep);
King Of Hearts (Out Of Joint and
Hampstead Theatre); *Gizmo Love* (ATC
and Assembly Rooms); *The School for
Scandal* (Salisbury Playhouse); *Cleansed*
(Headlong Theatre); *The Knight Of The
Burning Pestle* (Young Vic and Barbican);
In the Blue (Young Vic and Theatre 503);
Cloud Nine (Sheffield Crucible); *Richard
III* and *Measure for Measure* (Royal
Shakespeare Company); *Where Do
We Live* (Royal Court Theatre – Olivier
Award nomination for Most Promising
Newcomer) and *The Misanthrope*
(Chichester Festival Theatre).

Film credits include:
Kidulthood and *EMR.*

Radio credits include:
The Game of Love in Mornington Crescent.

Cast

Clive Francis
Argan

Jake Harders
Cleante

Clive's theatre credits include:
Never So Good (National Theatre);
The Dresser (Watford Palace Theatre);
The Woman Hater and *The Skin Game*
(Orange Tree); *Our Man in Havana,
Three Men in a Boat, The Hollow Crown,
Lavender Hill Mob,* and *Travels With
My Aunt* (Tour); *Loot* (Bristol Old Vic);
The Tempest (Nottingham Playhouse);
Entertaining Mr Sloane (Arts Theatre);
Gross Indecency and *Absolute Turkey*
(Gielgud Theatre); *Three Hours After
Marriage, Troilus and Cressida* and *A
Christmas Carol* (Royal Shakespeare
Company); *What the Butler Saw*
(Wyndhams Theatre) and *Single Spies*
(Queens Theatre).

Television credits include:
*The Queen, New Tricks, Pierrepoint,
Rosemary and Thyme, Reversals,
Longitude, Wycliffe, The 10%'ers,
Sharpe's Company, Lipstick On Your
Collar* and *Quartermaine's Terms.*

Stage adaptations include:
*Our Man in Havana, Three
Men in a Boat, The Hound
of the Baskervilles* and *The
Lavender Hill Mob.*

Publications include: *Laughlines;
The Many Faces of Gielgud; There
is Nothing Like a Dane!* and *There
is Nothing Like a Thane!*

www.actorclivefrancis.com

Jake trained at The
Grotowski Center, Poland.

Jake's theatre credits include:
Six Characters in Search of an Author
(Chichester Festival and West End);
Hobson's Choice (Chichester Festival
No 1 Tour); *Rope* (Watermill Theatre,
Newbury); *Cymbeline* (Cheek by Jowl
world tour – Rolex Mentor-Protégé
Award Nomination); *The Comedy of
Errors* and *Titus Andronicus* (Globe
Theatre); *Journey's End* (West End);
Professor Bernhardi, Rose Bernd and
Candida (Oxford Stage Company
– Ian Charleson Award Commendation).

Jake's theatrical debut was
aged 8 at the Liverpool Empire
in *Supergran - The Musical!*

Radio credits include:
The Picture Man.

Television credits include:
Beethoven, Wannabes and
Foyle's War.

Cast

Chris Porter
Bonnefoi, Monsieur Fleurant,
Doctor Purgeon

Chris' theatre credits include:
Victory (Arcola Theatre); *A Midsummer Night's Dream* (Creation); *Much Ado About Nothing* and *Bartleby* (Red Shift); *Gaslight* and *Table Manners* (Frinton Rep); *The Misanthrope* (Sevenoaks Playhouse); *Little Brother, Little Sister* (Kings Head Theatre); *Hard Times* (Compass); *Onysos the Wild* (Theatre 503 and Traverse Theatre); *Tartuffe* (Watermill Theatre, Newbury); *Someone Who'll Watch Over Me* (Globe Theatre Group, Warsaw); *Kalila Wa Dimna* (Maidan Theatre, Kuwait); *Angels Among The Trees* (Nottingham Playhouse); *The Night Before Christmas* (Riverside Studios); *Saints Day* and *The Road to Ruin* (Orange Tree); *The Art of Success* (Arcola Theatre); *The Dwarfs, The Local Stigmatic* and *Lakeboat* (Lyric Studio, Hammersmith); *The Winter's Tale* and *The Maid's Tragedy* (Globe Theatre); *Macbeth* and *Romeo and Juliet* (Tour).

Television credits include:
The Brixton Bomber, The Genius of Mozart, Footballers Wives, The Bill and *Bad Girls.*

Film credits include:
Beginner's Luck and *The Winslow Boy.*

Lucinda Raikes
Angelique

Lucinda's theatre credits include:
Don Juan Comes Back From The War (National Theatre Studio); *Rosencrantz and Guildenstern are Dead* and *The Children's Hour* (National Theatre); *Lost In A Mirror* (BAC); *Mad For Love* (Riverside Studios); *Life's a Dream* (Old Red Lion); *Cloud Nine* (Grace Theatre) and *Mary Stuart* (Union Theatre).

Television credits include:
The Thick of It, Cinderella, Freezing, Green Wing, Extras, Sensitive Skin, Casanova, 15 Storeys High, People Like Us, Raging and Tales of Uplift and Moral Improvement.

Film credits include:
In the Loop, Bright Star and *Special People.*

Cast

Brigid Zengeni
Beline

Brigid's theatre credits include:
A Christmas Carol (Rose Theatre,
Kingston); Macbeth (AFTLS, US
tour); Dr Faustus (Bristol Old Vic);
Three Sisters (Birmingham Rep);
Two Gentlemen of Verona and Julius
Caesar (Royal Shakespeare Company);
Oliver Twist (Lyric, Hammersmith);
The Wide Sargasso Sea (Citizens
Theatre, Glasgow); Phaedra
(Concentric Circles, national tour); The
Soul of Chi'en-nu (Young Vic Studio);
The Wedding (Southwark Playhouse);
The Winter's Tale (Royal National
Theatre); A Bedroom Farce (Frankfurt
English Theatre); Twelfth Night
(National Theatre Tour); Madame De
Sade (Riverside Studios); The Taming
Of The Shrew (Southern State Festival,
USA); The Legend of Pericles (Green
Belt Theatre and national tour); The
Mikado and The Pirates of Penzance
(New Vic, Stoke) and Passion Play
(Greenbelt Productions).

Television credits include:
Identity, New Tricks, Holby City, Silent
Witness, Inside Out, The Bill, William
and Mary, The Cry, A Touch Of Frost,
Active Defence, Casualty, Dr Willoughby,
The Greatest Little Store on Earth,
Holding the Baby, Wycliffe, and Beck.

Short film credits include:
Hospital Drama.

Brigid regularly reads for Radio 4's
Poetry Please.

Company

Roger McGough
Adaptor

Roger first appeared on stage at the Liverpool Playhouse in 1963 as a monk in John Osborne's *Luther* directed by Bernard Hepton. His first play *The Commission* directed by Peter James, was performed at the Everyman theatre in 1967.

Born in Litherland, he attended St Mary's College, Crosby before going to Hull University where he began writing poetry, while attempting his first translations of Molière. After four years of teaching he joined up with John Gorman and Michael McCartney to form *The Scaffold*.

The author of more than fifty books he is an Honorary Fellow of Liverpool John Moores University and an Honorary Professor at Thames Valley University, and has D.Litts from the universities of Liverpool, Hull and Roehampton.

In 2001 he was honoured with the Freedom of the City of Liverpool, along with Brian Patten and Adrian Henri, and in 2004 he was awarded a CBE for services to literature.

This is the second time Roger has adapted Molière's work, the first being *Tartuffe* at the Liverpool Playhouse in 2008.

Gemma Bodinetz
Director

Gemma Bodinetz took up her post as Artistic Director for the Liverpool Everyman and Playhouse in September 2003. Since then she has directed *The Kindness of Strangers, The Mayor of Zalamea* and *Intemperance* at the Everyman; *Ma Rainey's Black Bottom, Who's Afraid of Virginia Woolf? The Lady of Leisure, All My Sons* and *Tartuffe* at the Playhouse; and *Yellowman* on tour.

Gemma previously worked at The Royal Court Theatre, London, leaving briefly to assist Harold Pinter on *The Caretaker* before returning to co-direct *Hush* with Max Stafford-Clark. She then moved on to become a freelance director and Associate Director at Hampstead Theatre.

Gemma's other directing credits include: *Caravan* and *A Buyers Market* (The Bush Theatre); *Yard Gal* (Royal Court, London and MCC New York);); *Breath Boom* (The Royal Court, London); *Hamlet* (Bristol Old Vic); *Luminosity* (RSC); *Rosencrantz and Guildenstern are Dead* and *Four Knights in Knaresborough* (West Yorkshire Playhouse); *Paper Husband, Chimps, English Journeys, Snake* and *After the Gods* (Hampstead Theatre); *Shopping and Fucking* (New York Theatre Workshop); *Closer to Heaven* (West End) and *Guiding Star* (Liverpool Everyman and National Theatre).

Mike Britton
Designer

Mike trained in theatre design at Wimbledon School of Art, London.

Mike's theatre credits include: *Statement of Regret* (National Theatre); *The Vertical Hour* (Royal Court, London); *Noises Off* and *Doctor Faustus* (Liverpool Playhouse); *The Morris* (Liverpool Everyman); *That Face* (Royal Court, Upstairs and Duke of Yorks Theatre); *Don't Look Now* (Lyceum Theatre, Sheffield and Lyric Hammersmith); *The Winter's Tale, Pericles,* and *Madness in Valencia* (Royal Shakespeare Company); *A Midsummer Night's Dream, Coriolanus* and *Antony and Cleopatra* (Shakespeare's Globe Theatre); *Henry V* (Manchester Evening News Award for best design), *Mirandolina* (Manchester Royal Exchange); *Wuthering Heights, The Lady From The Sea* (TMA Awards for best design) and *She Stoops To Conquer* (Birmingham Repertory Theatre); *Period of Adjustment* (Almeida Theatre); *Tartuffe, The Gentleman from Olmedo, The Venetian Twins, The Triumph of Love* and *Dancing at Lughnasa* (Watermill Theatre, Newbury); *Walk Hard* (Tricycle Theatre); *Pure Gold* (Soho Theatre); *Nakamitsu* (The Gate Theatre); *Comfort Me With Apples* and *Glass Eels* (Hampstead Theatre); *The Three Sisters* (Abbey Theatre, Dublin); *Twelfth Night* (Theatre Royal Plymouth and tour); *The Comedy of Errors* and *Bird Calls* (Crucible Theatre, Sheffield); *John Bull's Other Island* (Lyric Theatre, Belfast) and *The Age of Consent* (Pleasance Theatre, Edinburgh and Bush Theatre).

Company

Conor Linehan
Composer

Conor Linehan has composed scores for theatres throughout Ireland and Britain.

Conor's theatre credits include:
Intemperance (Liverpool Everyman); Tartuffe and The Lady of Leisure (Liverpool Playhouse); Macbeth, Two Gentlemen of Verona, Edward the Third, Loveplay and Luminosity (Royal Shakespeare Company); Peer Gynt and Playboy of the Western World (National Theatre); The Wake, Saint Joan, The Colleen Bawn, Love in the Title, The Tempest, She Stoops to Conquer, The Cherry Orchard, Homeland and The School for Scandal (Abbey Theatre, Dublin); A View From The Bridge and Long Days Journey Into Night (Gate Theatre, Dublin); Everyday and Dublin By Lamplight (Corn Exchange); Antigone, The Crock of Gold (Storytellers); Mermaids (Coisceim Dance Theatre); Rebecca (David Pugh Ltd); Rosencrantz and Guildenstern are Dead and Four Knights At Knaresborough (West Yorkshire Playhouse); The Mayor of Zalamea (Liverpool Everyman); Carthiginians and A Dolls House (The Lyric Theatre Belfast) and Twelfth Night (Thelma Holt productions).

Conor also works as a concert pianist in which capacity he performs an extensive solo and chamber music repertoire.

Charles Balfour
Lighting Designer

The Hypochondriac marks Charles's fifth show at the Liverpool Playhouse following The Flint Street Nativity, The Lady of Leisure, The Tempest and Hedda Gabler.

Charles's other theatre credits include:
Now or Later, The Girlfriend Experience, The Ugly One (Royal Court, London); Loot (Tricycle Theatre); The English Game (Headlong); I'll Be the Devil (Royal Shakespeare Company); Ghosts, Baby Doll, Therese Raquin, Bash (Glasgow Citizens); The Weir (New Vic, Stoke); Christmas Carol (Rose Theatre, Kingston); Angels in America Parts 1 and 2 (Lyric, Hammersmith); Look Back in Anger, A Doll's House, A Christmas Carol and Son of Man (Northern Stage); Duchess of Malfi,

Don Quixote and Hedda Gabler (West Yorkshire Playhouse); Cleansed (Oxford Stage Co); Woyzeck and Witness (Gate Theatre).

Dance credits include: The Red Balloon (Royal Opera House) and 11 years as Richard Alston's main collaborator plus work with San Francisco Ballet, Birmingham Royal Ballet, Stuttgart Ballet, Rambert, Aletta Collins and Rosemary Butcher.

Opera and Musical credits include:
Saul (Opera North); Hagaromo, Writing to Vermeer, Thimble Rigging (QEH); Hair (Gate Theatre); Victory Over the Sun (Barbican Theatre) and The Rake's Progress (Aldeburgh Festival/London Opera Festival).

Future work includes projects with Opera North and Beijing Dance Academy.

Jason Barnes
Sound Designer

Jason has been involved with theatre sound for over 15 years, designing sound for productions throughout the UK. Jason was also Head of Sound and resident Sound Designer for Bristol Old Vic from 1999-2007.

Jason's theatre credits include:
Quadrophenia (Plymouth Theatre Royal and UK Tour); Enjoy (Bath Theatre Royal, UK Tour and West End); Once Upon a Time at the Adelphi, Noises Off and Dr Faustus (Liverpool Playhouse); Home (Bristol Old Vic Studio); We're Going On A Bear Hunt (UK Tour); What the Butler Saw and Alphabetical Order (Salisbury Playhouse); A Small Family Business and Enjoy (Watford Palace Theatre); Ma Vie En Rose (Young Vic); City of One and Through the Wire (Myrtle Theatre Company); Private Peaceful (Bristol and tour); Mother Goose, Aladdin-Genie in the Sky with Diamonds and Unprotected (Liverpool Everyman); Up the Feeder Down the Mouth and Back Again (Bristol Industrial Museum); A Streetcar Named Desire and Blues Brother Soul Sisters (Bristol Old Vic).

Jason was also Sound Engineer on Rapunzel for Kneehigh Theatre (UK tour and adaptation for the off-Boadway venue, New Victory Theatre NYC).

Company

Jacquie Davies
Costume Supervisor

Jacquie's theatre credits include: *Lost Monsters, Billy Wonderful, Mother Goose, Endgame, Eric's, Intemperance, The Way Home, The Morris* and *Port Authority* (Liverpool Everyman); *The Price, Our Country's Good, Tartuffe, Once Upon a Time at the Adelphi* (Liverpool Playhouse); *Vurt, Wise Guys, Unsuitable Girls* and *Perfect* (Contact Theatre, Manchester); *Oleanna* and *Memory* (Clwyd Theatr Cymru); *Love on the Dole* (The Lowry, Manchester); *Never the Sinner* (Library Theatre, Manchester) and *Shockheaded Peter* (West End).

Opera credits include work at: Scottish Opera, Buxton Opera Festival, Music Theatre Wales and Opera Holland Park.

Television and film credits include: *Queer as Folk, The Parole Officer, I Love The 1970's* and *1980's, Brookside* and *Hollyoaks.*

Ginny Schiller
Casting Director

Theatre credits include: *King Lear, Intemperance* and *The May Queen* (Liverpool Everyman); *Tartuffe* and *All My Sons* (Liverpool Playhouse); *The Winslow Boy* and *A Christmas Carol* (Rose Theatre, Kingston); *Home* and *Born in the Gardens* (Bath Theatre Royal); *Much Ado About Nothing, The Tempest, Romeo & Juliet, Twelfth Night, A Midsummer Night's Dream* and *Gigi* (Regent's Park Open Air Theatre); *Crown Matrimonial* (tour/West End); *Imagine This* (Theatre Royal, Plymouth); *The Giant* (Hampstead); *Far from the Madding Crowd, Hello & Goodbye, The Changeling, French without Tears, Someone Else's Shoes, Mother Courage, The Old Country, Hamlet, Rosencrantz and Guildenstern are Dead* and *Twelfth Night* (as Casting Associate for English Touring Theatre); *Stockholm* (Frantic Assembly); *Dancing at Lughnasa* (Lyric Theatre, Belfast); *The Last South* (Pleasance, Edinburgh Festival); *The Canterbury Tales* and *Complete Works Festival* (Royal Shakespeare Company); *Macbeth* and *How Many Miles to Basra?* (West Yorkshire Playhouse);

The Taming of the Shrew (Wilton's Music Hall); *Dr Faustus* and *The Taming of the Shrew* (Bristol Old Vic); *A Passage to India* (Shared Experience); *Macbeth* (Albery) and extensive work at Soho, Chichester and the Royal Shakespeare Company.

Television and film credits include: *The Kingdom, Notes on a Scandal, George Orwell – A Life in Pictures* (Emmy Award Winner), *The Bill* and *The Falklands Play.*

Radio credits include: *The Conflict is Over, The Leopard, Felix Holt the Radical, The Pickwick Papers, Tender is the Night* and *The Bride's Chamber.*

Lisa Spirling
Associate Director

Lisa trained at Royal Holloway University of London, LAMDA and the National Theatre Studio.

Credits as Director include: *Cotton Wool* (Theatre503); *Idiots of Ants* (Arts Theatre, Pleasance, Edinburgh and on tour); *Beowulf* (Storm on the Lawn, Theatre Royal Bath); *Can't Stand Me Now* (Royal Court Theatre, Reading); *Beauty and The Beast* (Jacksons Lane); *The Vagina Monologues* (The Pleasance, London); *No One Move* (Barons Court Theatre); *Gas & Air* and *New York Threesome* (Edinburgh Fringe and The Pleasance, London).

Credits as Assistant Director include: *Boeing-Boeing* (ACT Productions, Liverpool Playhouse and National Tour); *King Lear* (Headlong, Liverpool Everyman and Young Vic); *The Daughter* (The Wedding Collective); *1001 Nights Now* (Northern Stage and Regional Tour); *24 Hour Plays* (The Old Vic); *The Little Tempest* (National Theatre Education).

Lisa is the programming director at Theatre503 and artistic director of Buckle For Dust Theatre Company.

The Hypochondriac

Characters

Argan, *a hypochondriac*
Béline, *his second wife*
Angélique, *his daughter*
Cléante, *in love with Angélique*
Béralde, *his brother*
Toinette, *a servant*
Bonnefoi, *a notary*
Diafoirus, *a doctor*
Thomas Diafoirus, *his son*
Purgeon, *a doctor*
Fleurant, *an apothecary*

Act One

Scene One

As the house lights fade so does the music. During the sustained blackout, the silence is interrupted by a long fart. Stage lights come up as **Argan** *enters stage right, fastening his dressing gown and muttering to himself. He goes to his desk and resumes his accounts.*

Argan
> *Rien de tout, rien de tout . . .*
> *C'est fou, c'est fou . . . rien de tout!*

(He sits at desk piled high with unpaid bills.)

> Now where was I? 'Item of the twenty-second . . .
> To lubricate bowel and make it fecund.
> To scour gut until clean as a whistle,
> With abrasive enema of nettle and thistle.
> Administered with tube, long and rubbery,
> Thirty sols.' Thirty sols? That's daylight robbery.
> Monsieur Fleurant, your invoices are so polite,
> Poetic even, but as an apothecary you're a right
> Swindler. What's this . . . 'Item of the third of May,'
> Ye gods, five sols for sennapods? You must be joking.
> 'For rhubarb and rose-water infusion for soaking
> Long tube before full penetrative colonic irrigation, ten sols.
> For garlic and onion infusion for soaking
> Long tube *after* full penetrative colonic irrigation, twenty sols.'
> Monsieur Fleurant, that is out of the question.
> And so is this . . . 'Ear-drops to clear nasal congestion,
> Eye-drops to eliminate dandruff and scurvy,
> And dropsy-drops to prevent dropsy.' That's topsy-turvy,
> And at forty sols? *Mon dieu, trop cher.*
> 'As prescribed by Doctor Purgeon, a soporific
> Made from lettuce to help you sleep.' In fact, it did,
> But at a cost of fifty sols, well, that's horrific.
> In bed tonight I'll not get a wink of sleep
> Counting the cost of your expensive sheep.

He mimes trying to sleep.

'*Un franc, deux francs, trois francs, quatre francs . . .* '
I'm sorry Monsieur, twenty's plenty, more than enough
For a flask of mashed-up watery, salady stuff.
'Item . . . First of June, five sols for cleansing liver
    with vinegar douche.
Ten sols for cauterising piles with hot poker.' Ouch!
And what's this? 'To thin the blood, a cordial, fortified,
Of pomegranate, rabbit droppings, hand-washed and
    wind-dried,
Brandy, bull's testicles, etcetera, etcetera.' How much?
I'm mortified. Thirty? I'll give you ten and no more.
Monsieur Apothecary, what do you take me for?
I'm not made of money. If I wasn't at death's door
I'd send you packing. Can't you concoct some cure-all
    magic pill?
At this rate I can't afford to go on being ill.
I'll have a word with Doctor Purgeon in the morning,
    first thing.
Now where's that silly girl? *Ding ding! Ding-a-ding! Ding-a . . .*
A-a-a . . . ! That's all I need, a bout of sneezing!
I'll die of flu, this place is freezing. *Achooo!*
And where's that silly bell? . . . Ah . . .

He finds and rings the bell.

Toinette! . . . Toinette! Move me, I'm sitting in a draught!
Toinette, Toinette, are you deaf as well as daft?

He rings the bell furiously.

Scene Two

Toinette *rushes in, holding her head as if dazed.*

Toinette
    All right, all right, keep your hair shirt on.

Argan
What took you so long?

Toinette
Your wretched *ding dong*! It's like the crack of doom.

Argan
It's been an hour −

Toinette (*hands to head*)
Oww . . .

Argan
− since you left me alone in this room.

Toinette
Oww . . . oww . . .

Argan
Will you pay attention while I'm shouting at you?!

Toinette
Is there blood? There must be blood. I'm sure I'm bleeding.

Argan
I know *I'm* bleeding. Bleeding furious.
And why are you always so tardy?

Toinette
Don't be so grumpy, no need to get mardy.
When you rang I was on my knees a-scrubbing the floor
Up to me elbows in bubbles and soap.
I jumped up and cracked my skull on a cupboard door.
And do I get any thanks for my troubles? Nope.

Argan
So, you cracked your skull, skullking in the skullery?

Toinette
Yes, and it aches − can you spare me a pill?

Argan
Not at these prices, try vinegar and brown paper.

Toinette

Thanks, Jack.

Argan

Don't mention it, Jill. Now stop blubbing.

Toinette

Then tell me what you want
So I can get back to my scrubbing.

Argan

Move my chair. I'm uncomfortable,
I'm cold and sitting in a draught too.

Toinette

Do I have to?
Oh, all right.

He stands. She moves the chair. He crosses and sits.

Argan

Now go and boil a pan of water,
It's time for my next enema.

Toinette

Not another of those emenas.

Argan

Emena? Enema! Enema!

Toinette

Enema, nenema, nenema. Mark my words,
You'll have an enema too many one of these days.
It can't be good for you, all this irrigation.

Argan

Humph, you know nothing about my medication.

Toinette

One thing I do know. That Monsieur Fleurant
Has pumped so much water into you
It's a wonder the River Seine hasn't run dry.

Argan

It's a messy procedure, I'll not deny.

But the man knows what he's doing.
Why, he's fully qualified.

Toinette
Aye, as a plumber maybe.
Why, him and that Doctor Purgeon,
They're bleeding you dry.

Argan
That's enough! Show respect, some restraint.
You know nothing of my complaint.

Toinette
Yes I do. Complain, complain, complain,
That's your complaint. Complaining time and time again.
Complain, complain, complain . . .

Argan
Will you just shut up and fetch that water?

Toinette
Come shine or rain,
Complain, complain, complain . . .

Argan
Ah, what perfect timing, my dutiful daughter.

Scene Three

Enter **Angélique**.

Argan
Ah, Angélique, *ma petite chou*,
There's something of great import
I have to say to you. Your pulse will race,
Your heart flutter like a sparrow within your breast
When you hear my news. Which, as news goes, is the best.

Angélique
Dearest Papa, I am all agog.

Argan
> Then I'll begin . . . (*Clutches stomach.*) Oh, wait a minute . . .
> I'm just off to the bog.

He rushes offstage.

> Hang on, I'll be back in two shakes.

Toinette *and* **Angélique** *listen in silence. Sound of gurgles, long sigh of relief.*

Toinette
> One look at you, that's all it takes.

Angélique
> Oh Toinette, that is so unkind.

Toinette
> Yes, I'm sorry, take no mind.
> It's just your father, he drives me up the wall.
> Those charlatans Purgeon and Fleurant,
> They have him in thrall. They're imposters.

Angélique
> Yes, and a fortune it's cost us.
> But let us not talk about *mon père*,
> Let's talk about . . . *mon cher.*

Toinette
> Ah, who else? For six days now
> Cléante has been the sole topic of your conversation.

Angélique
> My world revolves around him! (*She twirls.*)

Toinette
> You'll make yourself dizzy.

Angélique (*still twirling*)
> He's adorable.

Toinette
> Is he?

Angélique (*stops twirling*)
O Toinette, fate arranged our meeting.
Don't you agree?

Toinette
Ah, *mais oui*.

Angélique
A love like ours is surely meant to be?

Toinette
Surely meant to be!

Angélique
So brave the way he leapt to my defence
When that brute accosted me?

Toinette
Most definitely.

Angélique
A gentleman from the tips of his toes
To the top of his noble head?

Toinette
Well said.

Angélique
And handsome?

Toinette
As a man can be.

Angélique
And charming?

Toinette (*losing interest*)
As a chestnut tree.

Angélique
And witty?

Toinette
As a bumble bee.

Angélique
And sexy?

Toinette
As a cup of tea?

Angélique
Toinette, you're teasing me.
Can't you see my emotional state?

Toinette
Sorry, I cracked my skull in the skullery
And find it hard to concentrate.

Angélique
Then concentrate now . . . Do you think he loves me,
Really loves me as much as he professes?

Toinette
Well, my guess is . . .
That he does. Although . . . and it happens, I've seen it,
He may *say* he loves you, but not mean it.

Angélique
Oh Toinette, 'twould break my heart
If what you say were true . . . But the letter?

Toinette
Oh yes, the letter he promised to write
Asking for your hand in marriage.
Then you'll find out soon enough
If he's a man of truth and honour
Or one of deceit and bluff.

Scene Four

Argan *re-enters with a spring in his step and sits.*

Argan
Ah, mission *accompli*!
Now come hither, child, and sit by me.

I have some unexpected news.
Someone has asked for your hand in marriage.

Angélique *jumps with glee.*

Argan
Aha, you jump for joy at the proposal.
That was easy. I suppose I'll
Tell the fellow you're as keen as mustard?

Angélique
Anything you say, Papa. I'm flustered
Of course, by the suddenness of events,
But I will gladly do your bidding.

Argan
Then I'll bid him hence.
You're a sensible girl, no kidding.

Pause.

But on the subject of your getting wed,
Your stepmother, it must be said,
Was vehemently agin the notion
And urged me to send you to a convent,
To a life of prayer and devotion.

Toinette (*aside*)
Oo, she would, the scheming hussy. She's vile.

Argan
But employing all my boyish charm and guile
I succeeded in talking her round
To my way of thinking. So now I'm honour bound.
I admit I have never set eyes on the man,
But he's soon to pay a call.
Not handsome by all accounts,
But straight-legged, they say, and tall

Angélique
Oh Papa, he is indeed handsome.

Argan
How do you know? Have you seen him?

Angélique
Well, Father, now that the marriage has been sorted
I will confide. We met by chance six days ago.

Toinette
Since when, she's been transported.

Angélique
Romance infused my very being.

Argan
Is he sensible and well-mannered?

Angélique
As you will soon be seeing.

Argan
Honourable?

Angélique
As any man can be.

Argan
Fluent in Latin and Greek?

Angélique
Pardon me?

Argan
Will qualify as a doctor in three days?

Angélique
Will he?

Argan
Didn't he tell you?

Angélique
No. Who told you?

Argan
Doctor Purgeon.

Angélique
Doctor Purgeon? Are they acquainted?

Argan

Acquainted? They're related –
He's Purgeon's nephew, that's all.

Angélique

Cléante and Purgeon are related?

Argan

I don't know who this Cléante is.
I'm talking about Thomas, your intended,
Who will soon be here on one leg bended,
Asking for your hand. Thomas Diaforius,
That's the boy's name. Son of Doctor Diaforius,
Who is the brother-in-law of Doctor Purgeon.
I'm simply delighted. In fact I'm euphorious.

Angélique

I feel faint.

Argan

Only this morning, Purgeon, Fleurant and I
Arranged the marriage. We shook on it.
And tomorrow the young man's being
Brought over by his father. Look on it
As a nice surprise. A young maiden's dream.

Angélique

A surprise made in Hell. I'm going to scream.

She runs off. Pause, then a loud scream.

Argan

Ah, the poor dear's over-excited, I can tell.
When she meets her intended, all will be well.

Toinette

Argan, what are you playing at,
To destroy your daughter's future just like that?
Can't you see, she's shaken to the core.
Marrying her to some shindleshanks – what for?

Argan

It's obvious, surely, you're not blind

To the state of my poor health? To find
Someone from a medical family to be my son-in-law!
Why, what ailing man could wish for more?

Pause.

I'm at death's door.

Toinette
Frappe, frappe.

Argan
Qui est là?

Toinette
Silly mon.

Argan
Silly mon *qui?*

Toinette
Silly monkey who cares for nobody but himself.
Cocooned in a world of imagined ill health,
He prefers the company of obsequious charlatans
To the family that surround and love him.
With the exception of Béline, obviously.

Argan
Was that a joke? If it was I didn't get it.
If it wasn't I didn't like it. Toinette, can't you see
How much easier my life would be
With experts on hand to cater to my needs?
To cool my brow when it's fevered,
To sponge my nose when it bleeds.
Lotions from Araby, ointments from China,
Champagne enemas – what could be finer?
To lubricate bones that are squeaking,
To massage joints that are creaking,
To plug any orifice leaking –
In a word, to be cared for, relatively speaking.

Toinette
All right, you've made your point, and clearly.

But it presupposes that you're ill. But are you?
Really?

Argan
Of course I bloody am. Do you think I like being bloody ill?
Being stuck inside all bloody day? Do you? Do you?
I'm a hypochondriac, is that what you're inferring?

Toinette
Your words, not mine, and there's no need for swearing.

Argan
All right, numskull, let me try a different tack.
Here's a foolproof way to get my money back.
Medical bills have cost me a fortune . . .
Fact: Doctor Diaforius has only one son.
Fact: Thomas will inherit everything.
Fact: Doctor Purgeon has no children.
Fact: his nephew Thomas will inherit everything.
Fact: when Angélique marries him
I'll be richer than my wildest dreams.

Toinette
Fact: she'll have nothing to do with your crazy schemes.

Argan
But she must. She will.
Doctor Purgeon has eight thousand francs in the bank,
Most of which was mine before I got ill.
'Tis only right and just.

Toinette
To sacrifice your daughter's happiness?
I'm nonplussed.
If you want my advice –

Argan
– which I don't.

Toinette
– you should let her marry whom she chooses.
Her mind is made up.

Argan
Whose is?

Toinette
Angélique's. Her mind is made up, her heart looks elsewhere.

Argan
Do I care? Why, her mind is like a bed, she can unmake it.
And if it means a broken heart, then I will break it.

Toinette
You are a fool, sir. And cruel to boot.

Argan
I am no fool, and to boot you would not be cruel.

He moves towards her.

In fact my foot is itching to make acquaintance with your
   bum,
And when I catch you I promise
I'll kick you from here to kingdom come.

Argan *leaves his chair and gives chase, his wild kicks being easily avoided by* **Toinette** *as she skips around the room in between the furniture.*

Attempting one final kick **Argan** *falls backwards to the floor in a yowling heap.*

Toinette *makes a run for it and exits through one door as* **Béline** *enters through another.*

Scene Five

Béline
My angel, my precious, what are you doing on the floor?

Argan
'Twas the fault of that Toinette, Satan's whore.
She chased me round the room, 'twas most annoyin',
Then she tripped me up and kicked me in the groin.

Béline

Lawksy!

Argan

No respect has she for her lord and master.
She makes my hackles rise and my heart beat faster.
She'll be the death of me. She must go.
Get rid of her or she'll send me to my grave.

Béline

Oh, poppet, don't take on so.
Toinette can be uppity, but all servants misbehave,
'Tis their nature. Little by little they hoard and they thieve,
Work less and less, grow bored and then leave.
But this one is not afraid of heavy toil,
She is neat generally and, above all, loyal.
In this day and age one must bear in mind
That good servants are hard to find.
So when dealing with a maid one can't be too careful.
Nevertheless I'll give her an earful . . . Toinette!

Toinette *runs in.*

Béline

You have some explaining to do.

Toinette

Moi?

Béline

Oui, vous.

Toinette

Pas toi?

Béline

No *patois*, no. We speak only the King's French,
Though in translation with liberties taken.
Now I want an explanation.
What have you done to my darling husband?
Why, he's all of a quiver.

Toinette
Perhaps a teeny worm is a-chewin' of his liver?

Argan *gasps.*

Toinette
Madame, his condition is due in no small part
To the fact that I spoke to him straight from the heart

Argan
You had no right . . .

Béline
You had no right . . .

Toinette
Than marry off his daughter to a doctor,
I said he'd be better off sending her to a convent.

Argan
You had no right . . .

Béline
You had *every* right.
The heavens would rejoice, should common sense prevail
And Angélique leave home to take the veil.
A life of chastity and meekness her soul would cleanse.
For the sins of the world she would make amends.
And the life of a nun can be fun, so they say . . .
In a quiet . . . lonely . . . holy . . . sort of way . . .
You had every right to voice your opinion, and I agree.
But my husband is upset, as you can see,
So apologise.

Toinette (*whispering*)
Mumble . . . mumble . . . mumble.

Argan
Louder!

Toinette (*shouting*)
Mumble, mumble, mumble.

Béline

Toinette!

Toinette (*sheepish*)

I am sorry, sir, if my behaviour offended.

Béline

That's better. And now this debacle has ended,
Help me put some cushions in his chair.
Here to make you comfy, it's Mummy Bear.

Toinette

And here to put you to sleep, it's Little Bo Peep.

She puts a cushion over his face and runs off.

Béline

There now, *cheri*, would you like a rug?

Argan

I'd rather have a hug.

When she obliges, her proximity arouses him to paw at her. She fends him off.

Béline

Now now, don't get yourself worked up, 'twill do you
    no good.

Argan

On the contrary, it will cure my aches and cleanse my blood.
Come, make an old man happy, slip out of your dress.

Béline

Oh, how I too long for your sweet caress,
But the effort involved would cause such stress
On your heart, your kidneys, your lungs, your brain.
Detumesce! Would a moment's pleasure be worth the strain?
In truth, you might expire, sex could prove fatal,
So I suggest we wait till
You're fit and well, then I'll satisfy your every desire.

Argan

You're right, of course, as ever you are,
My light in the heavens, my morning star.

You are the sun round which my moon and earth revolve,
And I hereby resolve, that when I die, as die I must,
Ashes to ashes, dust to dust,
To bequeath to you the whole of my estate.
And now I'll make a will, before –
(*He coughs for dramatic effect.*) – it's too late.

Béline

A gift from the grave? I find the idea chilling,
And so am willing to forfeit any claim.
For I married for love and not for gold,
To care for you should you grow old.
The thought of spending your money makes me morbid,
And of your dying soon? Why, heaven *for*bid.

Argan

Oh thou art blessed, thou truly art!
But time waits for no man, so let's make a start.
I asked you to seek some legal advice
From an honest man at a reasonable price.
A notary, perhaps, to help and to guide?

Béline

Now there's a coincidence, he's waiting outside.

Scene Six

Béline

Argan, this is Monsieur Bonnefoi.

Argan

And how long have you two known each other?

Bonnefoi

Since spring, when I first serviced Béline.

Argan

Pardon? What exactly do you mean?

Bonnefoi

Er . . . sorry, I mean, when I was able to do her a service –
Clear up a legal problem . . . Er, I was her brief.

Argan
Well, that's a relief.
And has she spoken of my fortune,
Which to her, I intend to pass on, whene'er I pass on?

Bonnefoi
She may have mentioned it, *en passant*.

Béline
Oh this macabre conversation, I cannot abide.
Forgive me, dearest, if I wait outside?

Argan
No, my love, I bid you stay.
Hear what this wise and honest fellow has to say
About my proposed bequest.

Béline
Then I do your will, for you know best.

Bonnefoi
'Tis my sorry duty, sir, to tell you that you cannot bequeath
    anything to your wife.

Argan
Why not?

Bonnefoi
Well, most illustrious sir . . .

Argan
Call me Argan, please.

Bonnefoi
Merci, and if I may resort to jargonese: 'Every region, every
city, town and village therein, has its own legal traditions,
which, though complicated, and oft outdated, override, in
many circumstances, the law of the land. Such a will as you
propose would be null and void here in Paris.' Such is the
opinion of my learned colleague, the Chief Justice.

Argan
That's damned peculiar.
Is he trying to make a fool of yer?

Bonnefoi

Pas de tout. He also counsels that there should be no
dependent children of the marriage, or indeed of any
previous marriage.

Argan

What a monstrous world this doth create.
Are you telling me a man cannot bestow his estate
Upon a wife who loves and cherishes him? 'Tis criminal.
Women'll be offended. Such a law should be upended.
Though your honesty is straightforward and well meant
I think I need a lawyer who could circumvent
The law. God's teeth. Ain't that what lawyers are for?

Pause.

Bonnefoi

Oui . . . et non. Yes . . . and no.

Argan

Ja . . . und nein? Vat are you *sein'*?

Bonnefoi

I'm *sein* . . . I'm sayin' that lawers – and don't get me
    wrong –
Though the icing on the legal cake,
Are wont to nit and pick, for the sake
Of long discourses. Which, of course, is
Damned expensive. My advice would be
To hire an adviser . . . Someone like me.

Argan

Well done, sir, you've talked me round
With your counsel, both clear and sound.
Consider youself hired. Now, what I need
Is for everything to go to Béline, and not my daughter.
Can that be guaranteed?

Bonnefoi

If I may resort once more to legalese?
That would be for the best.

Argan
Pray, be my guest.

Bonnefoi
Then might I suggest . . . making a will in favour of a
trusted male friend of your wife's, leaving everything to
him, until your death when all is transferred to her. At the
same time, your wife might put forward a number of
creditors, to whom a large number of bonds could be
made out. In turn, they would provide papers stating the
money belongs to her. Naturally, while still alive, you could
give her cash and any amount of gifts.

A howl from **Béline**.

Béline
I want nothing. *Rien de tout.*
I want nothing, *rien*, if I can't have you.
If you were to die I could not bear it.
I would follow you beyond the grave, I swear it.
A love like ours, passionate, pure and all too brief.
Inconsolable I, uncontrollable my grief.

Argan
Look at me, De Bonnefoi, ill, plain and boring,
And behold my wife, beautiful and adoring.
(*To her.*) But I'm not in the grave yet, so try to be brave.
Let us make out the will as Monsieur advises
And in my study, hidden behind panelling, a nice surprise is.

Béline (*brightening*)
Surprise! For me?

Argan
Twenty thousand francs –

Béline
For me?

Argan
– in gold.

Béline
Then let us not tarry.

She gets him out of his chair and rushes him out, or wheels him quickly off.

Argan
What's the hurry?

Béline
No hurry, darling . . . (*Resuming her dolorous composure.*)
'Inconsolable I, unconsolable my grief . . . '

Scene Seven

Toinette *and* **Angélique**.

Toinette
Argon is in his study with Béline
And a friend of hers, a smooth operator,
Lupine and lean, who can't wait to
Get his hands on your father's loot.

Sound of wood panelling being broken. Or could it be a wheelchair overturned?

Angélique
Zut! What's that appalling din?

Toinette
Sounds as if the ceiling's falling in.

Angélique
No, 'tis my world that collapses.
Happiness with Cléante perhaps is
Doomed to failure. Oh Toinette, let my father
Give away every sou, I don't care,
But what I need is a friend, loyal and true.

Toinette
Cléante?

Angélique
No, silly, you.

Toinette
Oh.

Angélique
To give me courage, to help me through
The dark times that lie in store.

Toinette
Dearest Angélique, isn't that what characters like me are for?
Uneducated, but gifted with common sense,
Cheeky and unafraid to give offence
To their employers. Forever cheerful and witty . . .

Angélique
And pretty!

Toinette
Ah, you make me blush!

Angélique
Now let's not beat about the bush.
Toinette, if you would be so kind
As to warn Cléante about my father,
And of the wedding plans he has in mind . . .

Toinette
Yes, and if I appear to be on Béline's side
In all of this, to be at odds with you, or chide,
Have no fear, 'tis all pretence,
In time my coarse naivety will make good sense.
So relax my dear, we will not be outwitted
By a father, health-obsessed, and a wife embittered.

End of Act One.

Act Two

Scene One

Toinette *and* **Cléante**.

Toinette
Monsieur, quelle surprise.
What brings you here, as if I couldn't guess?

Cléante
To see Angélique, and discover under what duress
She suffers at the hands of her father. Having been warned
Of this fateful marriage, I must show my hand.
Reveal my true intentions and make a stand.

Toinette
Stout fellow, but take care.
Go in fists flying, and you won't get anywhere.
She is watched at all times, and not allowed
To speak to strangers, or mingle in a crowd
Of young men, bushy-tailed and single.
In fact, it was only because an old aunt,
For reasons that remain a mystery,
Took us to the theatre to watch a play,
That you two met. And the rest, as they say –

Cléante
– *c'est histoire?*

Toinette
No . . . is history.

Cléante
Ah, but I am not here as her lovesick suitor.
As it happens, a friend of mine is her music tutor
And he's allowed me to take his place.
I can't wait, I tell you, to see my beloved's face.

Toinette
Then while you're waiting say a prayer
For here comes her father, *le malade imaginaire.*

Scene Two

Argan *enters and with fierce concentration walks up and down the room.*

Toinette
What are you doing, pray?

Argan
My exercises. Doctor Purgeon advises
I begin each day by walking across the room
Twelve times, from wall to wall.
Twelve times there and twelve times back.

Toinette
That's twenty-four in all.

Argan
Correct, although regarding direction, he didn't make clear.
Do I walk from here to there, or there to here?
Up and down or side to side? Longitude or latitude?

Toinette
Who gives a care? You decide.

Argan
Young lady, I don't like your attitude,
Nor your voice, which I find overbearing.
It beats like a drum and affects my hearing.
My body is a sensitive instrument,
To be played *pianissimo*, with the gentlest of chords.

Toinette
Bravissimo, and before you resume treading the boards
There's a gentleman who wishes to speak to you.

Toinette *signals* **Cléante** *to step forward.*

Cléante (*loudly and brightly*)
Good sir . . .

Toinette
Shhh . . . *pianissimo*, his body's a sensitive instrument.

Cléante

Er . . . ah, I sense it is . . .
What I meant . . . it is a pleasure to see you looking so well.

Toinette

So well? Hell's bells, the man's a corpse on legs, can't you
see?

Cléante

Well, to be honest, he looks to me
Exceedingly . . . to be honest, well . . . well.

Toinette

Then you are as blind as a pipistrelle.

Argan

She is absolutely correct. Spot on.
This poor body of mine is wrecked . . . rot*ton*.
What you see as rude health, in reality is frailty.
I have not long to live, but I will give
You some precious moments of the time remaining.

Toinette (*aside to* **Cléante**)

What a stoic! Heroic, generous and uncomplaining.
He eats like a hog and drinks like a fish,
Farts like a dog, he's a total disaster . . .
(*Aloud to* **Argan**.) But I couldn't wish for a better master.

Cléante

Good sir, if I might explain . . .
Your daughter's singing teacher, an old friend,
Being indisposed, proposed I come as a substitute
And tutor her. For she has a gift, that's his impression,
And he'd be miffed if she should miss a session.

Argan

Very good, quite right. Toinette, go and get her.

Toinette

But, sir, might it not be better
If I were to take the gentleman to her room?

Argan
What a strange idea to arrive at.

Toinette
'Twould mean they'd be in private,
And many rooms away. And in your present condition,
Where *pianissimo* is the order of the day,
It would give Angélique free rein
To sing *fortissimo*, without giving you . . . migraine.

Argan
Not at all. Why, to soothe the fevered brow
Music is by far the best bet.
Ah, and here she is.

Angélique *enters.*

Argan
Now go and see if my wife is dressed yet.

Toinette *exits.*

Scene Three

Argan
Angélique, your music teacher is unable to teach
So this fellow has stepped in to fill the breach.

Angélique
Good Lord!

Argan
What's the matter?

Angélique
Rien de tout.

Argan
Qu'est-ce que c'est? What's happened to you?

Angélique
An extraordinary case of déjà-vu.

Argan
> *Qu'est-ce que c'est?* What's happened to you?

Angélique
> An extraordinary case of déjà-vu.
> (*Unaware of* **Argan***'s puzzlement.*)
> Last night I had this awful dream
> Wherein this man forced himself upon me.

Argan *eyes* **Cléante** *suspiciously.*

Angélique
> No, not him, the man in my dream
> Forced himself upon me . . . but this man –

Argan *again looks at* **Cléante**.

Angélique
> No, not him, someone who looks like him –
> Came to my rescue and saved the day.
> You can imagine the shock, Father dear,
> To see him suddenly standing here.
> The person who's been in my thoughts all night.

Cléante
> I am honoured, Mademoiselle, to have inhabited
> Your thoughts throughout the wee small hours.
> To hear that we share the same feelings,
> That your fears and desires are ours.
> And I pray you will forever spread your dreams under
>   my feet,
> That I may tread softly on them because they are your
>   dreams.

Angélique
> Ah, poetry, pure and simple!

Enter **Toinette**.

Scene Four

Toinette
Oh sir, I take them all back, the aspersions I cast
On your future son-in-law. I see clearly at last
Why you chose him. Why, he's handsome
As a gargoyle and as sharp as a newly painted door.
He and his father Monsieur Diafoirus are in the hall,
Shall I bid them enter?
(*Confidentially*) Angélique, he is sure to please.
When you see him your heart will burst from your chemise.

To **Cléante**, *who is about to leave.*

Argan
Tarry, good sir, tarry.
My daughter has yet to meet the man she's going to marry.

Cléante
I don't wish to be in the way . . .

Argan
Stay. Observe love at first sight.
In matters of the heart I am always right.
Thomas is the son of a successful doctor
Who in time will help restore me to fitness.

Cléante
In which case I will be honoured to witness
Such a momentous meeting,
And a courtship, pre-arranged and fleeting.

Argan
In fact, you must come to the wedding
And bring her music teacher too.

Cléante
I would be greatly hon—

Toinette
Fanfare of imaginary trumpets . . .
Here they come, in all their glory!
Would you welcome please . . . the Diafoiri.

Scene Five

Diafoirus *and* **Thomas** *enter.* **Argan** *puts his hand to his cap without removing it.*

Argan
Forgive me, gentlemen, but Doctor Purgeon,
Of whom you may have heard,
Has advised me against removing this cap.
Bared, he warned, a head may suffer mishap after mishap.

Diafoirus
I would have given the same advice
For aren't we doctors both?
Having taken the same instruction
And the same Hypocritical oath?

Argan *and* **Diafoirus** *speak over and confuse each other during the following.*

Argan
Sir, you do me great honour
By visiting me here today.
And may I say from the very depths
Of my heart, how much, how very much,
How very, very, very much,
I would have wished to have visited you, *chez vous*.
But being an invalid, and who knows better
Than you, sir, the validity of what I'm saying,
Being an invalid, I am housebound.
However let me assure you that I am,
And shall remain, sir, entirely at your service!

Diafoirus
Sir, my son Thomas and I
Are greatly honoured to visit you here today
And to be welcomed warmly into the bosom of your family.
We look forward to the forthcoming alliance
With overwhelming excitement,
Happy in the knowledge that it will prove
Productive and beneficial to all parties.

And you may rest assured, sir,
Regarding all matters medical,
We are wholly and entirely at your service.

Best foot forward, Thomas, and present yourself.

Thomas *ponders his best foot, makes a choice, moves, changes mind,*
stumbles.

Thomas
Dear sir, I come to salute, love, cherish and honour you as
a second father, *to* whom I should be more indebted *to*,
than *to* my first father. For although he engendered me, and
from his loins did I spring, you sir, out of the goodness of
your heart, did select me. His by necessity, yours by choice.
To him am I indebted *to* for my visage and physique, but to
you I aspire to the grace of superior faculties of morality
and to the intellectual facilities of the mind. And may I
add, sir, on a personal note, that as I observe and admire
the fruit of your gorgeous loins . . . I mean, the gorgeous
fruit of your loins, I pray that when she and I conjoin, the
harvest will indeed be plentiful. As your future son-in-
waiting, I come today to extend this most humble and
respectful tribute. Yours faithfully, Thomas Diafoirus.

Toinette
Behold the work of the paraclete!
He has the gift of tongues, honeyed and sweet.

Thomas
Was that all right, Father?

Diafoirus
Optime, optime.

Argan (*to* **Angélique**)
Say something to the young man.

Angélique
Like what?

Whispering when appropriate:

Thomas
Do I have to kiss her?

Argan
Something to the effect of . . .

Diafoirus
After your second speech . . .

Thomas
Dear Madame, the gods, in their sacred wisdom, have deemed that you shall be the mother-in-law I never had, and I am delighted . . .

Diafoirus
Not that one!

Argan
That's my daughter, not my wife!

Diafoirus
The other one.

Thomas
Oh, shall I wait until the wife arrives?

Diafoirus
No, do the address to Mademoiselle.

Thomas
Ahem. Dear Mademoiselle, as the statue of Memmon sings when struck by the sun's first rays, so doth my heart sing when bathed in the radiance of your beauty. Botanists inform us that a flower named *Heliotropium*, from the Greek *helios*, meaning the sun, or heliotrope, a flower native to Peru, turns its face constantly towards the great fiery orb that is the sun. So also doth my face turn towards your great fiery orbs . . . those eyes. As a magnet vibrates and turns towards the pole, so doth my pole, when drawn towards your magnet. Allow me, Mademoiselle, to place my heart upon the altar of your charms, a heart whose sole ambition is to beat in time to the rhythm of your cycle and to sing your praises, while I remain forever, your humble and adoring servant. Yours sincerely, Thomas Diaf—

Diafoirus (*a hushed bark*)
> She knows who you are!

Argan
> How about that then, eh?

Toinette
> Words? Why, he can almost make 'em talk.
> And as for the voice, he'd make a wonderful town crier.

Cléante
> If he's as good a doctor as he is a speechifier
> Then surely, 'twould be a pleasure to be poorly.

Argan
> And now, as we are with salutations replete
> Let us all take the weight off our feet.
> Toinette, my chair!
> Well, Monsieur, 'tis plain to see
> Your son has impressed us mightily.
> You must be bursting with pride.

Diafoirus
> Not pride exactly, nor affection actually,
> But rather, with satisfaction. A quiet satisfaction
> That has matured over the years like a fine camembert.
> As a child he was unimaginative and uninquisitive,
> And to be fair, neither lively nor alert. However
> His lack of wit and high spirits proved a blessing
> In that he was never in trouble. Mischief held no sway.
> For him, low jinks was the order of the day.
> Why, he'd be there in the room and you'd never know,
> Content to sit in a dark corner rocking to and fro.

Warmed by the recollection, **Thomas** *begins to rock.*

Diafoirus
> A late developer, he didn't learn to read till he was ten.
> But then again, once he started . . . he found it hard going.
> By nature taciturn, he found the best way to learn
> Was through perseverance. That unsung virtue
> That is the bedrock of our class and our profession.

'Trees which grow slowly bear the best fruit.'
And as I'd always wanted him to become a doctor,
I could see that his slowness of comprehension
And natural aversion to new ideas would stand him in
    good stead.
At medical school he struggled, I must admit, but eventually
Took the bit between his teeth and . . . floundered hopelessly.

Thomas

But . . . *'Aqua cavat lapidem non vi sed saepe cadendo.'*

Diafoirus

Exactly, 'Water wears out the stone, not by force, but by
    falling often.'
After seven years he awoke as if from a coma,
Resat his resits and gained his diploma.

Murmurings of approbation.

Since then he has made quite a name for himself
In college debates. Unyielding as a Turk, he destroys
The opposition with the stubborn logic of a blunt scimitar.
Unflappable and rigorous, he will pursue any argument
Until it lies gasping for breath. But what pleases me most
Is that he accepts without question the ancient principles
Of medicine. Not for him these new-fangled ideas
Some quacks, who play on our fears, would have us believe.
That blood is pumped from the heart and circulated round
    the body –

Argan (*shocked*)

The heart is a pump? Simply monstrous!

Diafoirus

– When everybody knows, and I mean *body* –

His smug chuckle is echoed.

– That blood is kept in balance by the same four humours
That determine our health both mental and physical.

Thomas

And as for the scandalous book by that crazy Englishman –

Diafoirus
William Harvey by name.

Thomas
The very same: '*Exercitatio Anatomica de Motu Cordes et Sanguinis in Animalibus*'. Not only trash but treason.

Argan
Why, it stands to reason, your profession, good sir,
Is awash with charlatans and quacks
Who should be locked in stocks or stretched on racks.

Diafoirus
Spoken like a true Christian.

Thomas *takes a scroll from his pocket and presents it to* **Angélique**.

Thomas
Please accept with my compliments this thesis about the importance of the body's humours, which we all assume is common sense. 'Tis also writ in Latin. Do you have Latin?

Angélique
Toinette, do I have Latin?

Toinette
Not the old-fashioned kind.

Thomas
Though a work of medical science, it is worth a perusal.

Angélique
I'm sorry, but I must make a polite refusal.
Such erudition would be wasted on me.

Toinette
OK, you can foist it on me.

Thomas (*with enthusiasm*)
It is the first in a series of theses.

Toinette
Then I shall put it in the closet
Where the master keeps his faeces.

Thomas

My other interest is dissection,
And if Monsieur has no objection
I would like to take you one day to watch me dissecting
    a cadaver.
Of a female, of course, your modesty to preserve.

Toinette

Mam'selle, I'm suspecting, would *ra*-ver
Do without that carving palaver. What a nerve!

Diafoirus

And furthermore, in the interests of procreation,
I've had my son examined, and without hesitation
I can swear to the efficaciousness of his manhoodness.

All

Thankgoodnessness.

Diafoirus

Regarding your bloodline there is no cause for fretting,
No sooner wed, they'll be begetting
Healthy children, I'll be betting.

Argan

Excellent, and I'm betting your son
Will soon be employed at Court. Am I right?

Diafoirus

No sir. I would advise against treating the great and the good.
The general public are more accommodating.
They complain less, stand pain better,
And put up with waiting. The rich on t'other hand
Demand to be cured. If things go wrong, as they often do,
You can rest assured they're certain to sue.

Toinette

How inconsiderate! Isn't it the job of the doctor
Merely to write out prescriptions and collect huge fees
And up to the patient to make himself better. Who agrees?

Argan

We all do.

Diafoirus

To the letter.

Argan (*to* **Cléante**)

And now might be a good time, don'tcha think
For Angélique to sing for us. She has the voice
Of a nightingale, or is it a thrush?
Un oiseau, certainly.
(*To* **Angélique**.) Take your time dear, no rush.

Cléante

Une alouette, she has the voice of *une alouette.*
And we'd like to sing for you, a duette.
A scene from a modern operetta, entitled *The Caged Bird,*
A piece of improvisation, that neither Angélique
Or myself have ever seen or heard.
(*To* **Angélique**.) Here's your part.

Angélique

My part?

Cléante

Yes, take heart, we'll just play it by ear.
Eventually, I promise, all will come clear.
Look into my eyes, let your soul take wing
Open the box of your innermost thoughts, and sing.
(*To everyone.*) Excuse my voice.
Although I teach music, singing's not my forte.

Argan

Well, who'd have thought, eh? Is it a good story?

Cléante

Indeed. A tale of passion, as yet unrequited.
In the exciting opening scene, Tircis, a shepherd, rescues
Phyllis, a shepherdess, from the clutches of a cruel bully.

Argan

What's his name?

Cléante

I don't know.

Argan
Fabio? That's a good name.

Cléante
If you wish, Fabio, although we don't actually meet him
Because the action has moved swiftly on to the second scene
Wherein Tircis falls deeply in love with Phyllis.
But before he can declare his devotion they are cruelly
    parted –

Thomas
How many sheep do they have?

Cléante
I've no idea.

Thomas
I mean, do they look after the same flock or do they have
a flock each?

Cléante
Er . . . a flock each. Anyway, they are parted, and to
compound sorrow upon sorrow, Tircis learns that her father
has promised his daughter's hand to another, so he devises
a plan to visit her disguised as . . . er . . . disguised as . . .

Thomas
A sheep?

Cléante
Possibly. His intention is to hear from her own sweet lips
the feelings she has for him. With the help of her trusty
maid he gains admittance.

Diafoirus
A shepherdess with a maid?

Thomas
Her sheep must all have golden fleeces!

Diafoirus
Ha ha! Or collect golden eggs from geeses!

Guffaws all round.

Cléante

He has barely entered the house when who should arrive
but his rival, the man her stupid father wishes her to marry.
The man is obviously a buffoon, a dolt, nincompoop, and
his impulse is to throttle the life out of him. But caution
prevails, and instead Tircis is moved to song:

The fields are alive with those musical sounds
And those musical sounds I still can hear.
The baa-lambs and the birds
How I long to hear those words,
Those . . . three little words.
Those three little, magical, wonderful words.
Phyllis, O Phyllis, sing, sing . . . three little words . . .

Angélique (*after pause for thought, she sings, with passion*)
Three . . . little . . . words . . .

Cléante

That was lovely, my dear,
But not quite what I wanted to hear.
Unbutton your soul, be freer.

Angélique (*with more passion*)
Three . . . little . . . words . . .

Cléante

There was passion there aplenty
You gave me three, I wanted twenty.

Angélique (*resigned*)
Twenty . . . little . . . words . . .

Cléante

Enchanting, or *enchanté*, if I may,
If you please, Miss, or Ma'mselle, *s'il vous plait*,
Look deep into your heart, or *ton coeur*,
And sing to me, or *chante*, what is there.
For as shepherdesses go, or *va*, you are terrific.

Angélique

Your bilingual tongue confuses, not amuses,
Be more specific.

Cléante

Eh, *bien*. Take the wool from your eyes and see clearly.
I am Tircis, *you* are Phyllis. I love you dearly.

Angélique

And I you, I you, I you, I you, I you, I you,
I you, I you, I you, I you you you, I I I you you you,
I I I I I you you you you . . .

Cléante

And you, I you I, I you I you, I you I too,
You I you I you I you I too I I I you you you . . .

Cléante *and* **Angélique**

I you I you I you I you you you.
I I I you you you, you I you I you I too . . . (*Etc., etc.*)

Argan

Does this go on for very long?

Angélique

But what are we to do, pray?
Do, pray? Do, pray? Do, pray?
But what are we to do, pray?
Do, pray? Do, pray? Do, pray?

Cléante

Do, pray? Do, pray? Do, pray?
What do you mean, *ma chou fleur*?
Do say, do say, do say.

Angélique

Your rival and *mon père*
They will stop our love affair.

Cléante

Ma chere, ma chere, c'est vrai, c'est vrai,
But my rival is a juggins –

Angélique

A muggins –

Cléante

A noodle and a looby –

Angélique
A lopdoodle, a dunderhead, a pigsconce and a booby –

Cléante
A clinchpoop, a gobemouche, a snollygoster, a gongoozler –

Angélique
A lickspiggot, a fuzzdutty, a jobbernowl, an ass –

Thomas
It's highly amusing.

Cléante
– Who's in love with the sound of his own braying,

Thomas
But what are they saying?

Cléante *and* **Angélique**
Ee-aw, ee-aw, ee-aw, ee-aw, ee-aw . . .

Argan
Must say, I can't stand this modern music.

Diafoirus
What happened to tunes, I want to know.

Argan
The old folk songs, eh?

Music changes to an upbeat, folk style.

Cléante
One misty, moisty morning a-going to the fair
I met a pretty shepherdess with flowers in her hair.

Argan *and* **Diafoirus** *cheer up.*

I asked her if she'd help me find a needle in the hay
Buxomly she looks at me, and this is all she'd say . . .

Angélique
O fol de rol and fol de rol and fol de rol and fol de rol,
And fol de rol and fol de rol and fol de rol again.
I curtsied through the meadow, I curtsied down the lane –

Cléante
I cursed her and I chased her, and I caught her once again.
Verily, thou inflameth me, what chance a kiss? I pray –

Angélique
I looked at him coquettishly, and this is all I'd say:
O fol de rol and fol de rol and fol de rol and fol de rol,
And fol de rol and fol de rol and fol de rol again.

Cléante
O Phyllis, won't you thrill us, you know that I desire thee –

Angélique
O Tircis, your verses undoubtedy inspire me –

Cléante
Come live with me and be my love –

Angélique
My love, I'm hesitating –

Cléante
Gather ye rosebuds while we may, let's do it while we're
    waiting
O fol de rol and fol de rol and fol de rol and fol de rol,
And fol de rol and fol de rol and fol de rol again.

Argan *and* **Diafoirus** *look less cheerful.*

Cléante
Fol de rol and fol de rol and fol de rol and fol de rol,
And fol de rol and fol de rol and fol de rol again.
Fol de rol and fol de rol and fol de rol and fol de rol,
O fol de rol and fol de rol and fol de rol again.

Toinette *joins in, as does* **Thomas**, *unabashed.*

Fol de rol and fol de rol and fol de rol and fol de rol,
O fol de rol and fol de rol and fol de rol again. (*Etc., etc.*)

Argan
Stop! Stop! That's quite enough for one day,
Or, for an eternity, I should say.
Call that a play? I call it utter drivel.
Phyllis, why she's a hussy, and Tircis? Plain evil.

I mean, what daughter would speak like that
In front of her father? 'Twould shame me
To the very core. Pure nonsense. Show me the score,
Why! There are no words, only music.

Cléante
'Tis the latest invention, sir, and comes from Spain
A method of writing words into the notes.
Language encrypted within minims and quavers.
Let me explain . . .

Argan
O save us from your tedious explanations.
Begone, sir, and take with you your silly Spanish innovations.

Béline *enters.*

Scene Six

Argan
Gentlemen, I trust you will forget this charade
Of childish nonsense. As shambolic a parade
As I have ever heard or seen . . . Ah, Béline.

Béline
Dearest heart, my sweet.

Argan
May I introduce Doctor Diafoirus and his son Thomas,
As bright a button as you are likely to meet.

Thomas
Dear Madam, the gods in their sacred wisdom have deemed
That you shall be the mother-in-law I never had, and I am
    delighted–

Béline
And I am delighted too.

Thomas
– That you and I shall –

Béline
I'm sure we'll get along famously.

Thomas
– Be as two planets encircling the moon.

Béline
Won't we, Argan?

Thomas (*peevishly*)
Oh, she's interrupted the flow, Pater,
Now I've forgotten the words.

Diafoirus
Then save it till later.

Argan
I wish you'd been here earlier. Give diddums a kiss.

Béline
Poor baby. What did I miss?

Toinette
Not much. Long speeches that featured
A second father, a singing statue and a heliotrope.
Shiny bells tinkling on a load of old rope,
Followed by a duet that nearly caused a riot.

Argan
I'll not deny it. I'm still aquake with rage,
But, the formalities over, let us move on to the betrothal stage.
Angélique, take your future husband's hand
And pledge your troth. Let all here bear witness
To the birth of true love and await its growth.

Angélique
Oh Father, why the unseemly rush
Toward the altar? Why the need to push
Me into the arms of a man I scarcely know?
And in truth, don't want to.

Argan
Because I am your father, and what I say must go.

Angélique
> But with respect, I find him unattractive.
> I suspect we have absolutely nothing in common
> And I'd expect to be miserable and endlessly bored.

Toinette (*softly*)
> Well, that's put him to the sword.

Thomas
> But Ma'mselle, with due respect *aussi*,
> I find you easy on the eye,
> And though I won't deny you can be saucy
> And at times a trifle wilful,
> I propose we go ahead and wed. Why wait?
> For in matters of debate I am extremely skilful.

Angélique
> I am sure you are, sir,
> But courtship does not take place in the debating chamber.
> You'll find in love no trace of logic. And remember,
> To woo a maiden with diatribes and disputations unyielding,
> Would be an affront, 'twould stultify and limit her.
> Her heart will not be won by your wielding a blunt scimitar.

Thomas
> *Nego consequentiam*, a phrase that with consummate ease
> Demolishes, I fear, your hypotheses.
> *Quod erat demonstrandum.* Intellectually you can't compete,
> So accept my hand, admit defeat.

Angélique
> Never. You are crueller than I e'er expected,

Thomas
> Your reading of the classics you've clearly neglected
> For in those far off, enlightened days
> Matchmaking was conducted in more colourful ways.
> For a bride-to-be to be seen keen to leave home
> Was deemed unseemly, so he would remove her by force.
> And though thrilled and relieved, she would protest, of
>   course.

Angélique
Are you a savage at heart, sir,
Who would treat me so cruelly?
The days of dragging maidens off by the hair
Are past, well and truly.

Thomas
Savage though the passion in my breast,
Noble my intentions, I attest.

Angélique
Then learn patience – it is the sign of true love
To yield to the wishes of your beloved.

Thomas
An old chestnut which I have well covered.
Quite simply, *Ergo non posse concedere.*
Or if you prefer the Greek:
Ou sunkhoro de to ge tosouton kai ego. Luo tas pedas
Taramasalata, etc., etc., etc. Quod erat demonstrandum.

Toinette (*a loud whisper to* **Angélique**)
Now there's a college education for you.
Learning dead languages with which to bore you.
You'd be sure to find wedded bliss
Curled up in a box of knives as sharp as this.

Angélique
I am not dimwitted, and should be permitted
To make my own choice. Pity this poor damsel
For hers is an unheard voice!

Béline
Ah tragedy! But I hazard a guess
That sooner than later we'll find
That our damsel in this dress
Has someone else in mind.

Argan
I will not be led by the nose
I am her father and what I say goes.

Béline

Oh petal, don't force her hand
She could settle in a nunnery –
Now wouldn't that be grand?

Angélique

I know your little scheme, Madame,
You'd have me silenced by the cloth.
Drawn then to the flame of father's gold,
Like a fortune-hunting moth.

Béline

Outrageous and untrue!
Methinks I love your father more than you . . . do.

Argan

You are disrespectful, unkind and coarse.
My will will be done, even if I have to use force.

Angélique

Women marry for different reasons.
I will marry for love and be a faithful wife,
Live with my husband for the rest of my life.
So I will not choose in haste to repent at leisure.
Some get married to escape their parents,
And some, not for pleasure, but in the hope
That his death will bequeath them wealth.
They thrill to the shortness of his breath
As they pretend to restore his health.
In widow's weeds they weep bitter tears
But only in the public eye. In private
They plan their next campaign.
Marrying not for love but for commercial gain,
They move from one dead husband to the next,
Taking with them the spoils of war.

Béline

Angélique, you are making me vexed
This really is the final straw.
You think yourself superior, when you're not at all.
And pride, young lady, comes before a fall.

Thomas

There is an old Greek proverb that goes –

Met' en kakoisi met' en euestoi philei
Xunoikos eien toi gunaikeioi genei.
Kratousa men gar ouch homileton thrasos,
Deisasa d' oiko kai polei kakon.

Which roughly translated means – 'May I never share my
home with the female race, neither in time of evil nor in
pleasant prosperity! When things go well for her, her
boldness is unbearable, but when she is afraid, she is an
even greater evil for home and city.'

Toinette (*disparagingly*)

We know what it means.

All look at her in amazement.

Thomas (*disappointed*)

Oh.

Argan

I've had enough of arguments, bickering and yelling
And your attitude I find gross and repelling.
So it's down to this. In four days' time
You either marry this gentleman
Or you enter a convent. *Compris?*

Angélique

Oui.

She flounces out.

Argan

And don't worry, beloved, she'll submit to my will.

Béline

I'm sure she will. Ah . . . will.
That reminds me, I have business in town.

Argan

Of course, see the solicitor at once,
See if you can solicit a response.

Béline
   Adieu, my love!

Argan
   Adieu!

Scene Seven

Argan
   To think . . . that woman . . . to think that I am the idol
      she idolises.

Diafoirus
   Life indeed is full of surprising surprises.

Argan
   Before you take your leave,
   Perhaps you could take my pulse?
   Simply to confirm my worst fears.
   How long do I have? Days, months or years?

Diafoirus
   Such an invitation would be churlish to resist.
   Thomas, take hold of the gentleman's wrist
   And what do you deduce?

Thomas
   An eccentric pulse, regular but diffuse.
   Strong and then weak, it alternates,
   A tide of blood that rushes in and then abates.

Diafoirus
   And what does that signify?

Thomas
   The tide goes out, the pulse is low,
   The tide comes in, it's high.

Diafoirus
   Bene. I agree.

Argan
I confess, I'm all at sea.
In landlubber's terms, what does it mean?

Diafoirus
A malfunction of the spleen.

Argan
Are you sure? Doctor Purgeon said it was my liver
That was infected.

Diafoirus
Liver? Spleen? They're all connected.

Thomas
'Tis all intestinal in the final analysis.
What begins with an ache, ends in total paralysis.

Diafoirus
Roast beef I assume he prescribed?

Argan
Boiled!

Diafoirus
Excellent advice. Boiled or roasted,
The poison is killed off by *le boeuf*.

Argan
And how many grains of salt should I sprinkle on my *oeuf*?

Diafoirus
Six, eight, ten – always an even number.
When taking pills, however, always take an odd number.

Thomas
And not oval-shaped, but spherical.

Argan
Pray, what is the science behind such thinking?

Diafoirus
Numerical.

Argan

Ah, of course. Thank you both, until we meet again, *au revoir.*

Diafoirus *and* **Thomas** *leave.*

Scene Eight

Argan

I thought you'd gone. Where have you been?

Béline

Delayed by a scene on my way out
That will blacken your bile and inflame your gout.

Argan

I cannot wait. Elucidate.

Béline

Something you should be aware of.
Passing Angélique's bedroom, I saw the pair of
Them. Her and her so-called singing tutor.

Argan

In music practice engaged?

Béline

Practice of a different kind, I'd wage.
On his knees before her, raining kisses
On her hand outstretched.

Argan

Wretched girl! I understand now
Why she turned us down.
As for him, I'll kick him out of town,
The lecherous lout.

Béline

Better use your stick, petal, remember your gout.
He will have gone by now anyway.
And I must fly.

Argan
Yes, my love, goodbye.
Farewell . . . adieu and god speed, *auf Wiedersehen* and *ciao ciao, bambino* . . .

Scene Nine

As **Argan** *slumps in his chair after* **Béline** *exits,* **Béralde** *enters.*

Béralde
Dear brother, on such a beautiful day why are you slumped
in a chair?

Argan
Because I'm down in the dumps and the worse for wear.
I've a boil on my backside which is not amusing,
It's burst its banks and the pus is oozing.
My throat is burning, my fingers are itching,
My eyes are dimming, my testicles twitching,
My chin has doubled, my toes are twisted,
My ankles have swollen, my elbows are blistered,
My bladder's deflated, my hair's turning white,
I sneeze through the day and I cough through the night.
I am fast in decline and wracked with pain . . .

Béralde
Apart from all that, you're as right as rain?
Excellent! Because the reason I'm here is to talk about my
niece.
I have heard rumours that unsettle me.

Argan
Don't nettle me! That girl's a hussy, a conniving minx,
Who is not as clever as she thinks.
Because in four days' time our troubles will cease
When she enters the convent at Saint Sulpice.

Béralde
Echoes there, I detect, of Béline.

Argan

I am offended by your cynical tone.
Don't you think I have a mind of my own?
Have you no respect for your elder and better?
The constant sniping, the desire to upset her?
Béline, believe me, is goodness personified.
With Angélique she has tried and tried.
Never losing her temper, hardly a complaint,
Her patience would have tested a saint.
She is cheerful and modest
And yet you speak ill of her, have the gall
To imply that my wife hath me in thrall.
'Tis nonsense, and I'm sick of it. Sick . . . sick . . .

He rises from his chair and calls out.

Toinette! Stick! Stick!

Toinette *rushes in and hands* **Argan** *his stick. He hobbles out.*

Act Three

Scene One

Béralde *and* **Toinette**.

Béralde
I came to see my brother for a little tête-à-tête
And what do I get? Never seen him so upset or agitated.
Was it the call of nature? He could have waited.

Toinette
Yes, he'll be sitting on the toilet, I'll be bound.

Béralde
No, he'll be bound . . . not you.

Toinette
That's true.
Those calls of nature, normal to people like us,
He answers with fanfares and inordinate fuss.
But Angélique's welfare is our main concern.
His plans for her future we must strive to overturn.
So please, in the face of your brother's blindness
And his wife's transparent greed,
Don't desert your niece, in this, her hour of need.

Béralde
Never. And I would posit this:
His supposed ill-health and constant aggression
Centres on his worship of the medical profession.

Toinette
Then let us wean him off this obsession.
Devise a plan to undermine his belief
In false idols. Show them in a light unsavoury.
Open his eyes to their supercilious knavery.

Béralde
Bien sur. But how?

Toinette

Get rid of Doctor Purgeon for a start.

Béralde

But he's the family doctor, have a heart.

Toinette

And Fleurant, that pitiful epitome of a pathetic apothecary.

Béralde

Pithily put, very. We shall certainly have to do something.

Toinette

I have an idea, a tiny seed
That if nourished will flourish to suit our need.
Wish me luck.

Béralde

Bon chance!

She exits. **Argan** *shambles in.*

Scene Two

Argan

Ah, Béralde, I'm glad you're still here.
Will you help me into my chair, I'm tired with walking.
All aches and pains as is my norm.
And how are you?

Béralde

Oh, on reasonably good form.

Argan

Are you in good health?

Béralde

I don't know.

Argan

What do you mean, you don't know?

Béralde

I never think about it.

Argan

But you should, there may be something seriously wrong
with you.

Béralde

I feel fine.

Argan

Why, at this very moment, your brain fluids
May be about to seep from your nostrils and ears . . .
Your blood may be curdling like cheese . . .
Your bowels swelling like –

Béralde

Argan, that's enough!

Argan

But have you no fear of illness?
Of catching some dread disease?

Béralde

No. My only fear is the fear of catching hypochondria.
Now please, perhaps we could have our little chat.

Argan

What about?

Béralde

Oh, this and that.
And I would ask you not to lose your temper while we're
talking.

Argan

Certainly not.

Béralde

To remain calm and composed.
No shouting or waving your stick in the air,
Even should we disagree.

Argan

The thought would just never occur.
You know me.

Béralde (*softly*)

Oui . . .
Now, brother, why are you marrying your daughter
To a medic, the sight of whom she clearly cannot stand?

Argan

The reason is obvious, I'd have thought.
To have a doctor close at hand.

Béralde

And if she doesn't consent, it's off to the convent?

Argan

To have a nun for a daughter,
Why, 'twould be a spiritual feather in my cap . . .
Or should that be feather in my spiritual cap?

Béralde

Claptrap! To consign her under duress
Would not impress the Almighty.
To confine her against her will?
Well, you run the risk of eternal damnation.

Argan

Brother, I'm not enjoying this conversation.

Béralde

That vow of poverty she would make,
To remain as poor as a church mouse –
Well, you wouldn't blame Béline
Were she to sing and dance about the house.

Argan

You have never liked her. Nobody has.
I don't comprehend it.

Béralde

Then don't be offended if I make myself plain,
She's your angel of mercy purely for self-gain.

Argan *stiffens.*

Béralde
But let us not quarrel, after all I could be wrong.
Who knows? After the funeral, to prove she loved you all
  along,
She drinks poison, slits her throat and throws herself into
  the Seine . . .
Could happen.

Argan
Yes, I can see that.
The pain of my demise being too much to bear,
She cuts all earthly ties, impatient to join me . . .
(*Pointing.*) Up there.

Pause.

Except, wouldn't the poison run out of the slit in her
  throat, and . . .

Béralde
Argan, you are my brother and I love you,
But you have become a laughing stock.
Wheezing and complaining like an old crock
Twice your age. You are as strong as a horse
With a constitution like a bull. And yet you engage
A small army of quacks to try and kill you,
Who prescribe pills, piercings, purgings
And potions. Rub their hands, then bill you.

Argan
You just don't understand.
If it weren't for my loyal band of medical practitioners
Led by Doctor Purgeon, the outlook would be bleak.
He told me himself, the position is,
I would be dead within the week.

Béralde
The position is, you are alive in spite of them.
Doctors! God, I hate the sight of them.

Argan

So, you don't believe in medicine? An art,
Respected and accepted down through the centuries?

Béralde

No, I don't. The ones that I meet are grasping and
bumptious.
And the belief that one man can cure another is
presumptuous.
The workings of the body remain a mystery
That has defied man's curiosity throughout history.

Argan

Doctors know nothing then?

Béralde

Oh, they know their classics, how to terrify you in Latin.
Carbunculus, angina, convulsio, constipatio, scorbutus.
Diseases they can classify,
Like a lepidopterist can name a butterfly.
But as he can no more breathe life into the dessicated
Specimen on the table, can the doctor resurrect the dying
man.

Argan

But in times of sickness everyone runs to the doctor –

Béralde

An example of human weakness, not medical competence.

Argan

Then what should a person do if he feels sick?

Béralde

Nothing.

Argan

Nothing?

Béralde

Rien. Rest is the key. When you're depressed,
Deep rest is best. Let Nature itself cure the disorder.
You get caught in the rain. You sneeze – *ashoo!*

Your nose is blocked, you cough – *cough!*
Your chest is wracked with pain. What do you do?

Argan
Summon Doctor Purgeon post haste.

Béralde
Of time and money, a total waste.
He performs nasal irrigation, then you get undressed,
He scrapes your tongue and pummels your chest.
He doubles your pain at enormous expense.
You still suffer, what's the sense?

Argan
It's the quality of suffering, that's what you pay for.
It's more genteel, less intense.

Béralde
But time itself would heal.
It's our own impatience and fear that makes us feel worse.
Before the body can regain its balance and restore itself
We're reaching for our purse.

Argan
Like an ostrich, you bury your head in the sand.
Surely, there are occasions when even old clever-clogs,
Mother Nature, needs a helping hand?

Béralde
Doctors would have you believe it.
It gives them credence and we find it flattering.
I won't deny you'll find a smattering of the newly qualified
For whom the patient comes first.
But they'll cling to their books as they grow old,
Developing a thirst, not for knowledge, but for gold.
They talk of flushing and refreshing,
Of reviving and restoring, of improving and maintaining.

Argan
If they're curing, who's complaining?

Béralde
It is meaningless and boring.

They peddle vanity and you fall for it.
Mention a new complaint and you're all for it.
You wear illness like a new coat – it defines you.
When someone asks in all innocence 'How are you?'
You don't reply 'Fine, thanks.' That would be too polite.
You reel off a list of symptoms that goes on half the night.
All of them in Latin, gobbledygook and vague.
No wonder folk avoid you, like, dare I say it, the plague?

Argan

Disgraceful! If only there was a doctor here to refute you.
Face to face he could argue his case . . . then shoot you.
Merely a flesh wound, of course.

Béralde

Of course. But enough of despondency and gloom.
Brother, I thought a night at the theatre might clear the air?

Argan

A new play? By whom?

Béralde

Molière.

Argan

Molière! The one who makes fun of doctors?

Béralde

That's the one – *Le Malade Imaginaire.*

Argan

Wild horses wouldn't drag me there.
I've read the crits. All talk, no jokes, no naughty bits.
And Molière is on his last legs, or so I'm told.
At fifty-one he's past his best, and far too old.
Béline heard the rumour from someone in the cast
That tonight's performance could well be his last.

Béralde

Mmm. A packed auditorium is not the ideal place
To be rolling round the stage, staring death in the face.

Argan
> That play of his, *Tartuffe,*
> It was a disaster on a major scale.
> To ridicule religion goes beyond the pale.
> He should be praising priests and men of that class
> To ensure the Last Rites and a requiem mass.
> Tonight if he should pass from us
> He'll be sorry he was blasphemous.
> And doctors in the house, all stony-faced,
> Will look upon his dying with distaste.
> 'Get on with it,' they'll cry. 'Serves you right!'
> Demand their money back, then disappear into the night.

House lights up for interval.

Scene Three

Offstage we hear **Fleurant**

Fleurant
> *Frappe, frappe!*

Argan
> *Qui est là?*

Fleurant
> Enema –

Argan
> Enema *qui?*

Fleurant
> Enema at the gate.

Argan
> *Entrez!*

Fleurant *bustles in with a long tube, syringe, buckets and an irrigation machine which he proceeds to set up.*

Béralde
> What the deuce . . .

Argan
Excuse me, brother, it is time for my sluice –
Irrigation of the colon.
If you're shy, why not wait outside the door?

Béralde
I'm not squeamish, I've seen your arse before.
Your left buttock has a mole on.

Argan (*concerned*)
Does it? A mole? I must show Doctor Purgeon.

Béralde
Argan, can't you survive a few hours without being
Treated and tested, molested and pestered?
Give yourself a rest, send him on his way.

Argan
As you so rightly say,
Fleurant, pack away your gear and come back later.

Béralde
Much later. Perhaps next year!

Fleurant
And what gives you the right to interfere?
Monsieur, pray keep your manservant in line.

Argan
He is my brother.

Fleurant
That is no concern of mine. Now let me get to work, please.
For I am an enemanologist of great expertise.

Béralde
Enemanologist indeed. Be on your way!
And take your box of circus tricks with you.
For my brother there will be no more insertions,
No watery perversions, no more enemas
With venomous rubber snakes.

Argan
Oh for goodness' sakes!

Fleurant

How dare you? I am an apothecary of note
And deal with my clients on a one-to-one basis.

Béralde

Ah, so that's why you're not used to talking to people's faces.
Out!

Fleurant *gathers his stuff, muttering darkly.*

Fleurant

I'm going to tell Doctor Purgeon about this.
About insulting my profession and preventing me
From performing my duties. You'll be sorry. You'll see . . .
You'll see . . .

He exits.

Argan

Oh Béralde, I think you have gone too far, there was really
    no need –

Béralde

Argan, talk sense.
Missing an enema is of no consequence.
How are we going to cure you of this affliction,
A belief in medicine both costly and infantile?
Though in robust health, you're in denial.

Argan

It's all right for you to talk, you don't limp when you walk
Or wake up in the middle of the night and everything's dark.

Béralde

Open the curtains, welcome in the moon.

Argan

If you were in my shoes, you'd soon change your tune.

Béralde

So what exactly is wrong with you?

Argan

Ah, here's Doctor Purgeon!

Béralde
Talk of the devil.

Enter **Purgeon.**

Scene Four

Purgeon
I have just heard the most disturbing news.
That someone in this house sees fit to refuse
Remedies that I have prescribed.

Argan
Sir, it wasn't me, Sir . . .

Purgeon
The Greeks have a word for it . . .

Toinette
There's a surprise.

Purgeon
Hubris, meaning arrogance or pride.
A trait that we in the Faculty cannot and will not abide.

Argan
It was him, Sir.

Purgeon
I spent a great deal of time and effort
Concocting an enema based on an ancient recipe –

Argan
Don't think less of me –

Purgeon
The effect of which on your bowels
Would have been miraculous. Instead, catastrophe!

Argan
Ah!

Purgeon
> To send it back? Why, 'tis a slap in the face
> Of my profession, and in your case
> The punishment must be severe.

Toinette
> Hear, hear!

Argan
> It's all his fault –

Purgeon
> As you have so rudely refused my concoction,
> My only option is to sever my services.

Argan
> Sever your services? Never!

Purgeon
> Consider them severed.

Argan *gasps.*

Toinette
> He'd rather be tarred and feathered.

Purgeon
> You will receive an invoice for my services up to this date
> The prompt settlement of which I would appreciate.
> And when you find another doctor, or should I say, if,
> Your reputation having been sullied,
> I hope you show him greater respect,
> For he'll not be scorned or bullied.
> And as I no longer wish to be associated
> With your family in any way, here is the bond
> That was to be gifted on my nephew's wedding day –

He rips up the deed of gift.

Argan
> It was my brother, he's to blame –

Purgeon
> To pour scorn on my perfect enema,
> Why Sir, have you no shame?

Argan

I'll take it now, I'll take it . . .

Purgeon

I was coming so close to cleaning out your entire system.

Argan

Of all my ailments?

Toinette

List 'em.

Purgeon

Bowels grumbling, brain inflamed,
Kidney crumbling, bladder maimed,
Humours fetid, hearing impaired,
Spine decrepid, sight blurred,
Heart shrinking, lungs rheumy.

Toinette

Are we right in thinking, prospect gloomy?

Purgeon

Worse, far worse. It is bleak.
And though not given to prophecies
I predict that within a week
You will suffer the most fearful agonies,
Resulting in a condition known . . . as the Dreaded 'D's.

All

The Dreaded 'D's?

Purgeon

Decline and degeneration. That first, you will suffer
    dyspepsia –

Argan

Ah! I can't believe it!

Purgeon

From dyspepsia to dysentery –

Argan

Ah! I can't bear it!

Purgeon
From dysentery to diarrhoea –

Argan
Ah! I can't spell it!

Purgeon
From diarrhoea to dropsy –

Argan
Lawksy!

Purgeon
From dropsy to dysphagia, dysplasia, dyspnoea, dyspraxia, dementia.
And finally, to the most dreaded 'D' of all . . .

He pauses for dramatic effect.

Argan
Don't say it, don't say it . . .

Toinette
Dandruff?

Purgeon
DEATH!

He storms out, **Toinette** *following.*

Scene Five

Argan
Mon dieu! I am at death's door

Béralde
Frappe! Frappe!

Argan
Qui est . . . ? Oh shut up! Can't you see, I am destroyed.

Béralde
Nonsense. It's because you've challenged

His authority that Purgeon's annoyed.
He likes to think that your life is in the palm of his hand,
But now you've taken a stand
He declaims a litany of alliterative diseases.

Argan

The Dreaded 'D's?

Béralde

He's playing revengeful games.
A total fabrication, spewed from an imagination most cruel.

Argan

Four days, that's all I have. I am incurable –

Béralde

An incurable and unholy fool.

Argan

It's starting now, I can feel it, dyspepsia in my left foot . . .

Béralde

Right foot, surely?

Argan

Oh yes, it's the right . . .

Béralde

You have an opportunity now to turn over a new leaf
And rid yourself of doctors who bring nothing but grief.
Or at least find one less keen to dispatch you underground.
A l'enfer. Surely there must be one around?

Argan

Brother, that's unfair.

Béralde

Pardon, mon frère. Au paradis.

Toinette *enters.*

Toinette

Gentlemen, wonders never cease!
There is a doctor outside who wishes to see you,
And I must say you're in for a surprise.

Although Italian, he could almost be me in disguise!
Two peas in a pod, alike as two pins,
I swear to God we could be identical twins!

Argan
Then show him in.

Toinette *exits.*

Béralde
There you are, as one door closes, another opens.

Argan
And bangs you in the face!

Scene Six

Enter **Toinette**, *dressed as a doctor. Her speech is exaggeratedly Italian.*

Toinette
Signore, I was a-passing and heard a-moaning.
Perhaps I could be of service, for I am owning
A big knife. My speciality is amputation.
In Italy I have the *stupendo* reputation.

Argan
Who are you?

Toinette
Dottore Brontassore.

Argan
My name is Argan, I have four days to live, and this is my
    brother Béralde.

Toinette
I am from Padua, and I'm sad you are
Soon to depart this life.

Producing a long boning knife from her bag.

Should you require a bleeding before you go
My blade is as sharp as . . . a knife.

Argan

You are exceedingly like my maid.

Béralde

They are alike, certainly, but not the same.

Toinette

Ah, did someone call my name? *Scusi.*

'The Doctor' exits and **Toinette** *reappears.*

Scene Seven

Toinette

Oui?

Argan

Oui?

Toinette

What do you want?

Argan

I don't want anything.

Toinette

I thought you called.

Argan

No, I didn't.

Toinette (*mock-wearily*)

Oh, in that case I will get me to the scullery.

To the dirty floor and the heavy broom,

To the empty hearth and the darkened room,

To the scowling cat and the greasy pot,

To the existential bleakness that is my unhappy lot.

Argan

Jolly good, but before you do, stay awhile

And see how much this doctor resembles you.

It's uncanny.

Toinette

I know already. Didn't I point it out before?
Besides, he's old enough to be my granny.

She exits, leaving the two of them looking puzzled.

Argan

That girl is getting far too enigmatic for my taste.

Béralde

To my mind she has a brain that is going to waste.
I have met ladies at Court, even blue-stockings, I'm afraid,
With far less intelligence. Count yourself lucky to have such
    a maid.

Argan

Humph! But I reiterate my previous observation:
Can the doctor be an Italian close relation?
Same nose, same eyes, same lashes . . .

Béralde

Different moustaches?

Argan

Good point. And their voices have the same –
What's the word?

Béralde

Timbre?

Argan

No, it's an English word, er . . .

Béralde

Pitch? Tone? Resonance? Lilt? Cadence?

Argan

No, none of those.

Béralde

Timber?

Argan

That's it, the same timber.

Béralde
I've seen coincidences before, but only on stage.
In England, apparently, such devices were all the rage,
Comedy of Errors, *Twelfth Night* – twins were central to the
    farce.
But in real life?

Argan
My bottom!

Scene Eight

Doctor's voice off.

Toinette
Frappe, frappe!

Argan
Qui est là?

Toinette
Losta –

Argan
Losta qui?

Toinette
Si.

Béralde *opens the door and admits* **Toinette** *as the Doctor.*

Toinette
Prego, signori, my apologies.

Argan
C'est incroyable.

Toinette
You must *scusi* me for my audacity
But I was overcome with curiosity
To meet the hypochondriac whose fame is global

And examine perhaps, an invalid, both courageous and
   noble.

Argan
I am at your service, Sir.

Toinette
I notice you are staring at me. How old do you think I am?
Have a guess.

Argan
Oo, er . . . twenty-six, twenty-seven, maybe less.

Toinette
Aha! I am ninety.

Argan
Ninety?

Toinette
Si. I have encountered countless miracles as I have travelled.
The world has been my oyster and its secrets I have
   unravelled.

Béralde
He's amazing for ninety.

Argan
Oysters, that's his secret.

Toinette
O'er snow-capped mountains, from realm to realm.
Across oceans storm-tossed lashed to the helm,
Of a tiny ship I journeyed. Through jungles dense
And deserts immense, I put courage to the test,
For I had one quest in mind:
The secret of eternal life I was determined to find.

Argan
And did you?

Toinette
I didn't concern myself with medical trivia.
Heaven forefend! Broken bones that patients give yer

To mend. Coughs and colds and sniffling
Were symptoms I considered piffling.
Slight fevers, rheumatism and mild hysteria –
All deadly dull and wildly inferior.
Non. By nature impatient and imperious
I sought only illnesses that were serious,
Preferably with the patient tied down and delirious.
Good fevers, proper dropsies, lungs on fire,
Deep pleurisies, giant scabs to remove and admire.
In fact, the diseases I liked best
Were variations on *la peste*:
Chronic, bubonic, all shades of black,
I cured them all, I learned the knack.

Béralde
Bravo, Dottore! Bravo!

Argan
Perhaps you might consider giving me the benefit –

Toinette
Bene, if you give me a sample of your urine
When I return home to Turin,
I will test it for . . .

Argan
I thought you were from Padua?

Toinette
Oh, you're mad you are! As a hatter.
No, I was born in Padua but completed my studies
In Turin, where I now live. Does it matter?

Argan
No, no –

Toinette
Let's start with your pulse, let me have a feel.
Mmm . . . it's jumping around like an excited eel.
Who's your doctor?

Argan
Er . . . it is, er . . . was, er . . . Monsieur Purgeon.

Toinette
Never heard of him. Can't be very good.
And what does he say is the problem?

Argan
He says it's the liver.

Toinette
Not at all. It is your lungs.

Argan
My lungs?

Toinette
Si. And I, Dottore Brontassore from Pad . . . urin,
Will investigate the state you're in.
Now tell me your symptoms.

Argan
Well, I get these bad headaches . . .

Toinette
What did I tell you? Lungs.

Argan
And sometimes it's like a mist before my eyes –

Toinette
It's the lungs.

Argan
A burning sensation in my heart –

Toinette
Lungs.

Argan
And all my limbs feel tired.

Toinette
Lungs.

Argan
Pains in my stomach –

Toinette
Before or after a meal?

Argan
Both.

Toinette
Lungs.

Argan
And during.

Toinette
Definitely lungs.
What does your doctor advise in the way of diet?

Argan
Watery soup.

Toinette
Nincompoop!

Argan
Dry bread.

Toinette
Dunderhead!

Argan
Veal.

Toinette
Imbecile!

Argan
Calf's foot jelly.

Toinette
Off his trolley! Wine?

Argan
Watered down.

Toinette
The man's a clown.
You must drink your wine undiluted.

Lungs like yours are not suited to a diet so tasteless and
    thin.
So many things need changing I hardly know where to begin.
Good fatty mutton for a start,
Good fatty beef and a fatty pork tart.
Slices of cheese piled up on the plate
Will help the blood coagulate.
Waffles and pastries by the score,
Scoff rice puddings, then ask for more.
If you take my advice . . .

Argan
I will, I will . . .

Toinette
Then you can say goodbye to feeling ill!

Argan
Goodbye! Goodbye!

Toinette
Ah! And there is a recent medical breakthrough you might
    wish to try
Would you consider losing an arm and an eye?

Argan
An arm and an eye?

Toinette
Are you right-handed?

Argan
Yes.

Toinette
Then I'll be candid,
It is taking all the nourishment from the left.
Are you right-eyed?

Argan
Er . . . I don't know.

Toinette
Then I recommend that one is removed,

It's a question of balance, you see.
It has been scientifically proved,
You can take it from me.

Argan
Will it hurt?

Toinette
Only when you wave or blink.

Argan
In which case, I think –

Toinette
There's no rush. But it is time for me to say goodbye,
Or as we say in Italy, if you will allow . . .

Argan *and* **Béralde**
Caio!

Toinette
Adios!

As **Argan** *and* **Béralde** *exchange puzzled glances,* **Toinette** *exits.*

Scene Nine

Béralde
Mmm. That doctor does seem to be a clever man.

Argan
The trouble is, his reputation's made
In the gouging and amputation trade.
To losing an arm I'd be strongly averse,
And to lose an eye, what could be worse?

Offstage we hear **Toinette** *shouting and scuffling.*

Toinette
Gerroff! Gerroff! Yer dirty *dottore!*
That's enough. *A rivederci*, and don't come back!

An outer door slams, then **Toinette** *opens the door into the room.*

Really, what an outrage, such hanky panky at his age.

Argan
What's wrong?

Toinette
That doctor of yours wanted to feel my pulse.
One thing led to another . . . then he tried to kiss me.

Béralde
Wow! Ninety and still frisky.
(*Turning to* **Argan**.) Anyway, brother,
Let us return to the main business of the day.
Your daughter, my niece, how to clear the way
For her to marry the man of her choice.

Argan
Huh! I find that wholly amusing.
She has no choice, we do the choosing.
Having disobeyed and ignored us,
We commit her to a life of Holy Orders.
For her, *mon frère*, fasting, solitude and prayer.

Béralde
Was that the royal 'we' you used?
Or 'we' as in Béline and I? I am confused.

Argan
What do you mean?

Béralde
Preferring the shadows of illness to a healthy life
You become aggressive should anyone criticise your wife.
Let me put my cards on the table and speak freely:
You are an obsessive and unable to see clearly.
She is setting traps into which you will fall headlong.

Toinette
Nonsense, Sir, my mistress can do no wrong,
She is without deceit and loves my master dearly.

Argan
Tell him how she pampers me.

Toinette
Pampers –

Argan
And cuddles me.

Toinette
Cuddles –

Argan
Frets when we're apart.

Toinette
Frets –

Argan
How my illness breaks her heart.

Toinette
Breaks –
Behold! Our two lovers have climbed Mount Eros
And stand now on the very pinnacle.
Yet you, Sir, remain unmoved, cold and cynical.

Béralde
Huh! Mount Deception more like.

Toinette (*to* **Argan**)
Let us prove, Sir, how wrong he is.

Argan
How?

Toinette
Madam will be back soon
So stretch youself out and pretend to be dead.

Argan
Good idea. But what did I die of?

Béralde
You slipped and fell off Mount Eros.

Toinette
Sir, be serious.
Anything that will please yer,
An attack to the heart, a brain seizure . . .

Argan
Was I brave?

Toinette
Yes, yes, you died with a smile on your face.

Argan
Did I receive the Last Rites? Was I in a state of grace?

Toinette
Yes, and for pity's sake breathe your last!
Béline is in the hall and approaching fast.

Act Four

Scene One

Toinette *rushes* **Béralde** *into a dark corner to hide behind a settee.*
Béline *enters.* **Toinette** *puts her hands to her face like a Munch painting.*

Toinette
O mon Dieu, Non! Non!

Béline
Toinette, what is the matter?

Toinette
Madame, c'est votre mari, il est mort!

Béline
Talk properly.

Toinette
Your husband, ma'am, he is dead!

Béline
Dead? Are you sure?

Toinette
I heard him ding-a-ding, rushed in and found him on
    the floor.
I helped him into his chair.
He breathed his last, then died in my arms.

Pause.

Do you know what his last words were?

Béline
I couldn't give a monkey's.
Well, that's brightened up my day.
And cheer up, Toinette, it might never happen.
As for old miseryguts, he'd have wanted it this way.

Toinette

I thought you might be devastated?

Béline

Devastated? It's like being released from jail,
Offered shelter from a howling gale.
He was a storm in a bedpan, a floater in the sink,
He was the phlegm of my life, the bile and the stink.

Toinette

What a moving funeral oration.

Béline

Don't upset yourself, we have work to do.
No one knows about his death but you.
So let's get him into bed as if fast asleep,
For I have business appointments to keep.
Best the family think him alive until
I have had a chance to alter his will.
So first of all I will need his keys . . .
You take the head and I'll take the knees.

As **Béline** *and* **Toinette** *try to lift* **Argan** *from his chair, he sits up.*

Argan

Not so fast!

Béline

Aaaaggghhh!

Toinette

Heavens to Betsy!

Argan

So this is how you love me, you snake.

Béline

It was a joke . . .

Argan

Your phlegm, your stink, your bile, am I?

Béline

Expressions of love . . . I . . . I was in a state of shock . . .
Inconsolable I, uncontrollable my grief!

Argan
> For years I have been deceived and abused
> And having witnessed your touching eulogy
> I will mend my ways without fail.
> For there are lessons to be learned, I think.
> May you end your days in jail, or floating in a sink!

Béline *exits hurriedly as* **Béralde** *watches from behind the chaise longue.*

Argan
> Ah, the wicked things she said, that cruel laughter!

Béralde
> Well, brother, better you learned the truth about her now,
> Than in the hereafter.

Toinette
> Pssst, I hear Angélique coming – let's do it again.

Argan
> Oh no, I couldn't bear the strain
> Of hearing my beloved daughter speaking ill of the dead.
> Couldn't Béralde take my place as a corpse instead?

Béralde
> It wouldn't be the same.
> It's her feelings for you we are putting to the test.
> Now get back in your chair – Toinette knows best.

Scene Two

Enter **Angélique** *to* **Toinette**'s *wail of grief.*

Angélique
> Toinette, what is it?

Toinette
> *O ma petite, mon maître gentil, ton père, il est mort, il est mort!*

Angélique
Speak properly.

Toinette
Oh my child, my kind master, your father, he is dead, he
is dead!

Angélique
Aaagh!

Toinette
Look, there he is. He was his jolly self until moments ago
When, whoosh! Death struck a fatal blow.

Angélique (*rushing to him in tears*)
Oh Father, don't die, don't die.
O God, don't let him die. This can't be true.
Father, I have never loved anyone as I loved you.
And yet I made you angry, as you so often told me.
Did you scold me with your last breath?
Was my wilfulness the cause of your death?
Oh Daddy, forgive me, forgive me!

Scene Three

Enter **Cléante**, *who rushes to* **Angélique**'s *side.*

Cléante
Angélique, what has happened?

Angélique
Behold my father. Lifeless, as cold as stone.
With no one to comfort him, he died alone.
I felt his spirit calling but I arrived too late.

Cléante
My love, my poor love, what a cruel twist of fate.
In the knowledge that I had been maligned
I came to persuade him to change his mind.
On my knees I would entreat him, and pray
That pity would soften his heart this day.

But that heart is deaf and my voice unheard.
Struck dumb, our happiness now caged like a bird.

Angélique
Cléante, should you think of marriage, think not of me.
I renounce the world for ever, and set you free.
Daddy, if against your wishes I stood in the way,
Then one wish, at least, I promise to obey.
I will take the veil, and each day in silent prayer
Repent for the sorrow caused. This I do swear.

Argan (*sitting up*)
Dearest daughter!

Angélique
Ahhhh!

Argan
Fear not, sweetheart, I was only pretending.

Angélique
Thanks be to God –

Toinette
– For this miraculous happy ending.

Argan
I am overjoyed to hear your paeans of love so respectful
For a father, who too often was harsh and neglectful.

Angélique
Then, Father, since Heaven has your life restored
In thanksgiving, could one favour you afford?
If Cléante, my one true love, I cannot wed,
Don't force me into a marriage that I dread.

Cléante
Sir, open the cage, behold the crestfallen dove.
Open your heart, and let free the bird of love!

Argan
I will, by God, I will . . .
If from this charade, one lesson I have learned
It is to reward fidelity, and courtship hard-earned.

Pause.

With one proviso . . . .
That Cléante becomes a doctor, why didn't I think of it
   before?
I'd be happy then to accept him as my future son-in-law.

Cléante
I accept without hesitation, in fact, I have a small confession,
I have longed to be a member of that august profession.
And not for money, for I'm not greedy,
But the chance to help the poor and needy.
To visit hovels where the stench repulses
And wash their sores and treat their ulcers.
To deliver babies, cure rabies and scabies.
To use my new-found God-given power
To comfort those who, in their darkest hour,
Look death in the face and walk bravely to it.

Angélique
Darling! That's enough – don't overdo it.

Béralde
Brother, I have an idea, why not review your own position,
By taking the oath and becoming a physician?

Argan
Too old to embark on such a mission. Too long in the tooth.

Toinette
Nonsense, you'd cure yourself in no time.
'Physician heal thyself!' You'd be illness-prooth . . . proof.

Béralde
And you wouldn't have to study, or go to school.
When it comes to anatomy you're nobody's fool.
You've taken every medicine good or bad,
No patient could be greedier.
Is there a disease you haven't had?
Why, you're a walking encyclopaedia.

Argan
But I have neither Latin nor Greek.
If I consulted myself . . . what language would I speak?

Toinette

Once you've donned the cap and gown
Those classical terms will flow.
I was under an Italian doctor once, so I should know.
Which reminds me . . . I must go.

Toinette *winks at* **Béralde** *and leaves hurriedly.*

Béralde

Ah, *comprende*! Cléante, if you wouldn't mind
Popping outside, where I believe you'll find
Our friend the *dottore*, be kind enough to bring him in.

Argan

That oyster-munching old goat from Turin?
The smooth amputator? Brontassore?

Béralde

Yes, and not only a *dottore*, but a *professore*,
Who has the qualifications, I saw 'em, that we need
To confer your degree with decorum and speed.

Angélique

Oh Father, my excitement I can hardly contain –
A chance for you to pause, to begin your life again
Without Béline, the cause of your imaginary pain.

Scene Four

Enter **Toinette** *disguised as Brontassore, accompanied by a* **Quartet**
of eminent medics, consisting of the actors who played **Béline**,
Purgeon, Fleurant *and the* **Diafoiri**.

Toinette

God bless all here!

Quartet

Amen.

Toinette

By the powers invested in me, by the Powers that be,
I come to confer an honorary degree.

Quartet

By the powers that be, we all agree,
He comes to confer an honorary degree
We all concur, he will confer
An honorary, honorary, honorary degree.

Argan (*relieved*)

Is that all there is to it?
Don't I have to do anything?

Toinette

Questions of a medical nature, we have prepared.
Answer correctly and you'll pass.

Argan

But I'm scared.

First

Don't be, you'll come top of the class.

Second

That chronic anxiety about your own health –
Will be the key to success and guarantee wealth.

Third

Remember the symptoms, the disgusting cures –
Reel off the names and the degree is yours.

Argan *braces himself for the challenge.*

Toinette

How would you scour gut until clean as a whistle?

Argan

With abrasive enema of nettle and thistle.

Quartet

Bene, bene respondere.

Fourth

In what would you soak long tube *before* anal intrusion?

Argan

In rhubarb and rose-water infusion.

Quartet
Bene, bene respondere.

Fourth
And *after* it's been taken out and shaken?

Argan
Garlic and onion, if I'm not mistaken.

Quartet
Bene, bene respondere.

First
To clear nasal congestion?

Argan
Eye-drops.

Second
Dandruff and scurvy?

Argan
Ear-drops.

Third
Dropsy?

Argan
Dropsy-drops.

Quartet
Bene, bene respondere.

Toinette
For flatulence caused by overeating,
What remedy would you prepare?

Argan
An empty plate, perhaps.
Une salade imaginaire?

Quartet
Benissimo, benissimo.

Fourth
And how would you cleanse the liver?

Argan
With a vinegar douche.

First
And how would you cauterise piles?

Argan
With a red-hot poker.

Quartet
Ouch! *Bene, bene respondere.*

Second
And a cordial to thin the blood?

Argan
I know just the thing, it's fortified −

Second
Good.

Argan
− With pomegranate, rabbit droppings, hand-washed and
wind-dried,
Brandy and bull's testicles.

Third
How many?

Argan
Bulls? Just the one. Balls? Just the two.

Quartet
Bene, bene, respondere.

Fourth
This chap's a marvel, let us give thanks.
Bid him welcome into our glorious ranks.

First
Professore, may I suggest, without further delay −

Second
That he takes the oath and this very day −

Third

We confer his degree honor*ararary.*

Quartet

Bene, bene respondere.
Three hearty cheers . . . Hip, hip, hooray!

Toinette

Merci, messieurs,
And to mark the solemnity of the occasion
Let the furniture be rearranged,
Lighting subdued and the music changed.

The stage reflects these directions. **Argan** *has great difficulty in keeping up with Brontassore.*

Toinette

Repeat after me . . .

Argan

After me –

Quartet

Not yet!

Argan

Sorry.

Toinette

Ego, Arganus, swear in solemnibus . . .

Argan

Ego, Arganus, swear in solem . . .

Toinette

– That as a *novum membrum* of this *professio dignus* . . .

Argan

– Omnibus, that as a *novum* . . .

Toinette

I will *abidum* by the *regulare* –

Argan

– Member of this . . . *professes* . . .

Toinette
Institutare by the *concilium sapienti, molto et glorioso* –

Argan
– Oso . . .

Toinette
Et witnessi per doctores et professores qui hic assemblibunt est.

Argan
– *bunt est.*

Toinette
I now pronounce you, Doctor Argan.

Applause all round. Lighting and music changes as the **Quartet** *step forward.*

Toinette
And remember . . .

First
Make sure your patient pays up front –
In case of early *exeunt.*

Second
Once his cash is in your purse –
Who cares if he grows worse and worse.

Third
When a man stands before you, naked and weak,
Stifle a smirk at his wretched physique.

Fourth
Try not to ogle when a maiden undresses,
Mumble in Latin, that always impresses.

First
Remember what Aristophanes teaches –

Second
When in doubt, use a handful of leeches –

Third
If he's a pain in the bum – down the back of his breeches.

Fourth

Fingers crossed when giving a diagnosis –

Third

And the nastier the medicine –

Quartet

The larger the doses!

Toinette

As a doctor, and the saviour of the human race,
Remember medicinal compound is most efficacious in
    every case.

All

Most efficacious in every case!

Argan *steps forward and is lifted up by the company.*

Argan

Thank you, and God bless you, one and all,
For giving me back my health and my sanity.
This feeling of well-being will stay with me
For the rest of my life. I am transported with joy!

Curtain.

Printed in the USA
CPSIA information can be obtained
at www.ICGtesting.com
LVHW020852171024
794056LV00002B/498

9 781408 123850